LONGING FOR GOD

Prayer & the Rhythms of Life

Glandion Carney & William Long

Foreword by Steve Hayner

INTERVARSITY PRESS
DOWNERS GROVE, ILLINOIS 60515

InterVarsity Press® is the book-publishing division of InterVarsity Christian Fellowship®, a student movement active on campus at hundreds of universities, colleges and schools of nursing in the United States of America, and a member movement of the International Fellowship of Evangelical Students. For information about local and regional activities, write Public Relations Dept., InterVarsity Christian Fellowship, 6400 Schroeder Rd., P.O. Box 7895, Madison, WI 53707-7895.

Cover photograph: Tony Stone Images/Roger Wood
ISBN 0-8308-1665-8

Printed in the United States of America ∞

Library of Congress Cataloging-in-Publication Data

Carney, Glandion.
    Longing for God: prayer & the rhythms of life/Glandion Carney &
William Long.
        p.   cm.
    ISBN 0-8308-1665-8 (alk. paper)
    1. Bible. O.T. Psalms—Meditations.   2. Desire for God—
Meditations.   3. Spiritual life—Christianity—Meditations.
4. Devotional calendars.   I. Long, William Rudolf, 1952-
II. Title.
BS1430.4.C37   1993
223'.206—dc20   93-41899
                                                            CIP

---

15   14   13   12   11   10   9   8   7   6   5   4   3   2   1
05   04   03   02   01   00   99   98   97   96   95   94   93

To Gloria Golden
February 18, 1946—September 10, 1991
a person who taught us what it means
to live in the Psalms and
how to love God in the midst of suffering

Foreword by Steve Hayner   5

Acknowledgments   7

Introduction   9

PART 1: LONGING FOR GOD   15

1 PSALM 63 *Longing for God*   17

2 PSALMS 42—43 *Thirsting for God*   25

3 PSALM 84 *Home*   33

PART 2: LIVING WITH DISTRESS   41

4 PSALM 102:1-11 *Alone*   43

5 PSALM 130 *Waiting*   50

6 PSALM 39 *Rediscovering God*   56

7 PSALM 51 *Guilty*   63

8 PSALM 55 *Attacked!*   70

9 PSALM 44 *Rejected*   78

10 PSALM 69:1-12 *Sinking*   86

11 PSALM 69:13-36 *Climbing Out*   92

12 PSALM 88 *The Abyss*   99

PART 3: LEARNING TO TRUST GOD   107

13 PSALM 90 *Our Eternal Home*   109

14 PSALM 139 *Searched and Known*   117

15 PSALM 121 *Trust for the Journey*   125

16 PSALM 46 *God Our Refuge*   131

17 PSALM 37 *Don't Worry—Learn to Trust!*   137

18 PSALM 27 *God Our Light and Our Salvation*   145

19 PSALM 91 *The Warrior Is the Lover*   152

20 PSALM 23 *The Shepherd Psalm*   159

21 PSALM 40 *Out of the Pit*   165

PART 4: LOVING TO PRAISE GOD   175

22 PSALM 33 *Reasonable Praise*   177

23 PSALM 116 *The Joy of Being Heard*   184

24 PSALM 8 *Majesty*   190

25 PSALM 126 *Dreaming*   196

26 PSALM 65 *Tapping the Abundance of God*   202

27 PSALM 146 *Praise Forever*   208

28 PSALM 100 *Shouting for Joy*   214

29 PSALM 67 *In Ever-Growing Circles*   219

30 PSALM 150 *Praise as a Way of Life*   224

Appendix: Questions for Study and Reflection   229

Foreword

Praying the Psalms is not easy. Neither is using them in public worship. Even though *psalms* means "praises," these outbursts of the soul are filled with anger, fear, depression, and deep longing for justice and vengeance or for mercy and hope. The language is sometimes rough, the sentiments harsh. Yes, the praise is sometimes bursting with joy, the poetry sublime. But if we skip over the despair and pain to read only the victory and the joy, we miss the power of the Psalms and our worship becomes impoverished.

The Psalms were not written by nice people. But they were written by honest people, people who could tell God exactly what they felt and what they wanted him to do. They could look at all the junk in their souls and the mess in their world and tell God about it without fear that he would be offended. They knew God better than that.

Bill Long and Glandion Carney have done us a tremendous favor by showing us the rhythms of the Psalms and how they correspond to the ups and downs of our souls. The four themes that Bill and Glandion trace—yearning, distress, trust and praise—are keys which unlock the psalm writers' relationship with God and open the way for us to read the Psalms without skipping the parts which seem so embarrassingly unspiritual.

Glandion and Bill are richly qualified to guide us on this journey into the Psalms. They have walked through the valley of despair, looking within themselves for fresh resources to face a life and a God who do not fit our expectations. Glandion wrote of his own pilgrimage in *Heaven Within These Walls*: "The journey into the inner life is more a journey into God than into self. . . . The hunger for spiritual experience is God-induced. But it can only be satiated through the inner life of intimacy with God."

How could the psalmists shout and shake their fists at God and still live? How can Christians today read and claim these visceral prayers as their own? Because God himself invites us to. No, he *insists* that we do. He does not want us to clean up our act first, then come to him with devout and genteel phrases. No, either we come to him with everything, or we don't come to him at all.

We can't fool God. "Nothing in all creation is hidden from God's sight. Everything is uncovered and laid bare before the eyes of him to whom we must give account" (Hebrews 4:13). So we might as well tell God flat out who we hate, what we lust after, what we don't like about the way he runs the universe. We can confess our self-pity, our suspicions and our reluctance to trust him. And we can celebrate our victories with whoops of joy, our steps of faith with transparent glee. God likes it that way.

But that is so hard. We'd like to, but we are so self-conscious, so inhibited by formal patterns of worship, so afraid to offend. And so dishonest. That is where the Psalms help us. They show us authentic lives of faith, moving from vague longing after God through the distresses of life with tentative steps of faith to the full gladness of hearing God's yes! It's all there. Bill and Glandion will help you see it, and you'll be glad you did.

Steve Hayner
President
InterVarsity Christian Fellowship

Acknowledgments

We are grateful for the support and encouragement of many people throughout this project. We are thankful to InterVarsity Press and its editorial director, Andrew Le Peau, for his timely and thoughtful help in shaping this book. We are thankful to our wives, Marian Carney and Judy Steele, who have followed our work with interest and displayed constancy, love and support, not simply in this project but over the many years we have spent together. Finally, we express our gratitude to Marion Greeley, the efficient, helpful and accurate office manager of InterVarsity Missions Fellowship in Portland, Oregon, who prepared the text of the psalms for use in this book.

Introduction

This book is designed for individuals and groups who want to deepen their spiritual lives. It is intended for those who would like to have a regular time to read, meditate on and discuss the Scriptures and their lives but who, for some reason, have not consistently done this. Though anyone might find this book useful, it is especially written with *busy* people in mind—people who already have a lot of commitments and are afraid to take on more, but who know that they *need* to take a few minutes each day to read, pray and think about the Scriptures and their lives.

We all know the pressures of life in our times—two working-parent (or single-parent) families, intense days, demands on us from several angles at once, competitiveness (from the early years on), and the struggle to keep personal and family life together. These pressures convince us of our need to do something *each day for ourselves*, that is, to give attention to our own *spiritual nurture*. This is written for the person who does not want to put off any longer the regular cultivation of the spiritual life.

This book is meant as a practical guide to the spiritual life—a guide that will give structure to your study of the Scriptures and encourage your reflection on your faith and life. We write from the conviction that the Scriptures, when carefully read, shed great light on our way and give meaningful comfort and guidance to our lives today. Our hope is that you will use this book as a tool to help you establish a regular practice of reading, thinking about, praying over and writing your reaction to Scripture.

Our Theme

The idea that dominates this book is that a study of the Psalms can help us restore our balance or regain our spiritual rhythms. Each of us tries to establish or discover our rhythms in life. When we have our rhythms, we perform well, even amid enormous challenges. Yet we lose our rhythms so often and so easily. We become out of sync with ourselves, with our God, with our families and with the world around us. We become people we don't like, and our life takes on a kind of desperation or clumsiness that makes us and others uncomfortable. We long to regain our spiritual rhythm, but we're unsure how to do so.

Our goal for *Longing for God: Prayer and the Rhythms of Life* is to help you discover or regain your spiritual rhythms and balance, and find your true strength in God. We feel that the discovery and recovery of healthy spiritual rhythms does not come easily and effortlessly. But it is worth the effort.

We have divided thirty psalms into four categories or movements. These movements take us, in the course of one month, from our daily yearnings and fears to our praise of God as the integrating focus of life. We will study four movements of the spiritual life: longing for God, living with distress, learning to trust God and loving to praise God.

We begin with longing for God because each of us spends so much time yearning for a variety of things: acceptance, security, understanding, love and peace. Each day is a day of yearning. So we will begin this book where our daily life begins.

Yearning, however, opens us to the joys and disappointments of life. Often the latter seem to outweigh the former. So we need to study distress and how we live with it. We open our arms and sometimes we are embraced, but sometimes we are slapped in the face. The movement of distress helps us understand how we react when we have been slapped, when the trouble comes, and how we can continue to hope when we have been disappointed so often.

Some of us choose to remain in distress or disappointment. But the key to regaining spiritual balance or healthy life rhythms is to learn to trust God anew with our lives. Can we trust God and people even *after* the distress and betrayal has hit? The purpose of the third section is to deal directly with that question.

Finally, we turn to the last movement: loving to praise God. We cultivate good spiritual rhythms when we learn to praise God for life. Part four is designed to help us consider what praise means and how to make it a daily reality for us.

How to Use This Book

This book is meant for individual or group study. Each chapter begins with a psalm. This is usually followed by a reflection or story that is keyed to the theme of the psalm. Then comes an exposition of the passage. The expositions are of two types: thematic and sequential. A thematic exposition scrutinizes *a few leading thoughts* from the text. A sequential exposition tries to follow *the psalmist's thought process* as he writes. Each kind of reading has advantages, but the goal for both is for you to examine your life with the help of the biblical text and our exposition. We have deliberately kept our expositions brief, especially as the book nears its close, so that you will feel free to stop, reflect on *our* presentation of the issue, and perhaps make some of the biblical phrases or thoughts *your* own.

Following our exposition is a brief prayer to help you personalize some major themes of the chapter. For thirteen of the chapters we have included, as an appendix, study questions for individual or group use. We provide thirteen sets of questions so that those who use this book for group study or an educational program will have material for one full quarter of the year. We have also included these thought questions as an invitation for you to do some writing of your own on the Psalms. They are questions for those who are not afraid to think deeply about faith and feelings about life.

We recommend that you take between fifteen and thirty minutes for each chapter. Go at your own pace. Don't feel that you have to grasp *everything* for the exercise to be useful. Enter with an air of expectancy, and you will find that God is there, waiting to help you understand his Word and establish helpful spiritual rhythms in your life.

A Personal Word

Two people have written this book. We both feel, however, that our collaboration has been so close on nearly every chapter that we speak with one voice. Therefore, when we speak personally in this book we will often use the word *I.* This doesn't mean that we have both experienced each story; it means that we both embrace the truth of which the *I* speaks.

Yet we are two distinct people, who came to this project for different reasons and who were deeply affected in the writing of this book, by each other and by the circumstances of our lives. I, Bill, am a professor of history and government at a small Christian college in rural Kansas. When I moved to Kansas in 1990, I took up a new field (having previously taught religion at a college in the Pacific Northwest) and a new setting (rural instead of urban). The transition to a new field and a new setting was difficult for me. Because I had to spend considerable time reequipping myself, I took little time to continue my Scripture studies. My sense of alienation slowly grew until I wondered if I had any spiritual or intellectual center at all.

It was in this context that Glandion, whom I had met in 1990, suggested we do a study of the Psalms and use our personal experiences of joy and distress to help us read and apply the Psalms to our lives. As we talked together, the idea for this book grew. Longing, distress, trust and praise were all powerful experiences in my life as we studied the Psalms together. I can say, thanks to God, that the writing of this book has helped *me* regain my own spiritual rhythms.

I, Glandion, had just finished leading a six-week ministry tour to South Africa in the summer of 1991. I took ten African-American students and ten Caucasian-American students to visit, learn about and try to understand the nature of ministry in Soweto and other black townships in South Africa. The pain of poverty, alienation and injustice we witnessed was so severe, and the insistent questions of the students as to why this was happening were so intense, that I began to wonder myself about the goodness of God and whether reconciliation among people could ever take place. I wept as we visited a graveyard for children and saw three thousand graves of those little victims of a brutal system.

When I returned to the States, I came face to face with the fact that a dear friend, to whose memory this book is dedicated, was dying of cancer. She was only forty-five years old. She was a vibrant Christian, a mother of five children, and was wasting away before me.

After her death in September I began to feel as if I had been pummeled by life. God seemed so distant. I had lost any sense of spiritual balance or rhythm. I became deeply depressed and felt that my life was ebbing away from me. Since Bill and I had agreed to do some thinking about a book on the Psalms, I opened my Bible and began to read. Never before had the Psalms gripped me with such power. I began to identify with David in his yearning, distress and doubts. As I read, silently and aloud, a new and clear sense of balance and rhythm began to return. My life began to be renewed. That sense of renewed focus and rediscovered rhythms has strengthened in me as the project has moved through every stage.

As you read this book, may you too be refreshed and renewed through God's word in the Psalms.

PART ONE

◊

LONGING FOR GOD

◊

ONE

◊

PSALM 63

LONGING FOR GOD

A psalm of David. When he was in the Desert of Judah.

¹O God, you are my God,
   earnestly I seek you;
my soul thirsts for you,
   my body longs for you,
in a dry and weary land
   where there is no water.

²I have seen you in the sanctuary
   and beheld your power and your glory.
³Because your love is better than life,
   my lips will glorify you.
⁴I will praise you as long as I live,
   and in your name I will lift up my hands.

⁵*My soul will be satisfied as with the richest of foods;*
with singing lips my mouth will praise you.

⁶*On my bed I remember you;*
I think of you through the watches of the night.
⁷*Because you are my help,*
I sing in the shadow of your wings.
⁸*My soul clings to you;*
your right hand upholds me.

⁹*They who seek my life will be destroyed;*
they will go down to the depths of the earth.
¹⁰*They will be given over to the sword*
and become food for jackals.

¹¹*But the king will rejoice in God;*
all who swear by God's name will praise him,
while the mouths of liars will be silenced.

*I*n the Academy Award-winning film Amadeus *there is a scene where the lesser* Viennese composer, Salieri, reflected on why Mozart's music was so powerful. He said, with a combination of jealousy and wistfulness, that what characterized Mozart's music was such a sense of longing and yearning, such an unfulfilled desire that cried out through his music. It seemed as if Mozart was hearing the very voice of God and was striving with every fiber of his phenomenal genius to express musically what he had heard from God. He was a man who longed for another world, and his music was the result of that yearning.

The key to the life of Christian discipleship is to learn how to yearn and then to learn how to focus our yearning. A wonderful image of this phenomenon may be found in the story of the burning bush (Exodus 3). Moses is tending his flocks by Horeb, the mountain of God, when he turns aside to see a marvelous sight. A bush is burning, but it is not being consumed. From this apparently contradictory observation, Moses hears the voice of God calling to him. The word of God comes from the burning bush.

The bush may be symbolic of many things, but one of its meanings may be applied to us: we, like the burning bush, need to burn and not be consumed. That is, we need to burn with a desire for God, a hatred of oppression and every kind of injustice, a longing to see the word of God and the work of God performed in our generation. Yet often when I burn I am consumed, or, in the language of today, I become "burned out." I become so involved in things that I become consumed by them. I become so consumed by my desires—desires for money, prominence, sexual expression, change—that I am overcome and rendered useless.

When this happens, I have lost my balance, and I often then flee to the other extreme. I flee to indifference. I have seen how great a toll desire exacts in me, so to preserve peace and a sense of stability in life, I withdraw. I stop longing. I lose whatever heat I had and become cold indeed. Horrible images of beatings, killings, war, poverty, illness and brokenness can flit across the television screen and I remain passive, unconcerned and inert.

The key to Christian discipleship is to learn how to burn without being consumed or, in other words, to long without being overcome and immobilized. I need to learn to maintain my fire, my commitment, my longing even when I come close to burning out. I need to maintain that fire even when entering the deep freeze of unconcern seems most inviting. I fly to the extremes of burning consumption or frozen immobility. I need help, divine help, to achieve a balance, an equilibrium, a rhythm that keeps me longing and burning but does not consume me. I need to keep on loving even when love has been painful, to keep on hoping even when hope has been dashed before my eyes, to keep on believing in people even after they have let me down time after time, to keep on believing in myself even after I feel that I've failed at things most dear to me.

My spiritual journey, then, begins with yearning. My longing may, at first, be unfocused yearning. It may just be an ache deep within for wholeness or understanding. It may also have a greater focus to it: goals I want to reach, relationships I want to cultivate or heal, recognition I crave and feel I deserve. So, I long. The psalm I have chosen to start these reflections is about longing. We will spend three days on longing, for unless we clarify the nature of our longings, we will be unable to achieve spiritual balance or life-giving rhythms.

David's Longing

The first line of this psalm illumines the path of our whole journey. "O God, you are my God, earnestly I seek you." These ten simple words capture the essence of our initial step. First, David starts with a general cry to God. He simply says, "O God." I can't hear the tone of his voice, but it is a general cry, the plea of a heartsick and longing person who knows that salvation lies outside of himself. "O God" is a cry that I need to be able to make. It is not exactly a confession of faith in God; it isn't a declaration of discipleship. Rather, it is a call from the depths of my being, where deep calls to deep, a call that captures in its intensity all the tangled webs of my sadness, sickness and yearning. "O God" must be my first words. They come from desire. They are directed outside of myself. They can be said with desperation or anger or calmness. They need, however, to be said. Spiritual balance begins when I recognize that the first cry I make in the morning is really a cry for God. "O God" means that I instinctively recognize that the source of my life and the fulfillment of my needs come from God. "God" takes me no further than that, but the cry gets me on the right path.

Crying for God or calling to God brings me outside of myself. I need to be delivered from the mind curved in on itself, from the self absorbed with the self. There certainly are depths of soul that I need to touch and unexplained actions or feelings that I would be foolish to ignore. But, ultimately, there is no deliverance in life through self-absorption.

If I focus my attention solely or largely on myself, the result, paradoxically, is confusion and not control. My life and my mind are to find their reference point in their rest in God. The mind focused largely on itself is a mind tumbling out of control, like a car careening over the icy surface of a highway. It cannot stop, and it cannot control where it goes. The mind focused on itself becomes like an astronaut walking in space who for some reason has lost his tether. Thus, I tumble farther and farther toward the outer reaches of the universe with no guide, tether or way of regaining control. The way to put valuable self-examination in a proper context is to control it with daily cries to God.

Walt Whitman may have written, "I celebrate myself and sing myself," and I, too, may exalt in the wondrous complexity and grandeur of the human God has made. But I also need checks on the endless self-absorption that our culture encourages. Crying out to God will not assure that I will be immediately delivered from the pits of my despair, but it tells me that my true health is found outside of myself, in the grace and comfort of the living God.

Second, David continues with a *personal* cry to God: "You are my God." He makes a huge advance with these words, by willingly claiming God as his God. This is not an easy step to take. To say "God," all I need is a voice. But to say, "you are my God," I need something else. I need a sense that God can be trusted. In addition, it means that I believe God is concerned about my condition. Many people will confess that God exists and that he even hears their cries, but fewer really believe that this God is personally interested in their lives.

What does it mean to say, "You are my God"? It means I agree that God deserves not just my cries of desperation but also my will and my heart. Another psalm captures this perfectly: "I said to the LORD, 'You are my Lord; apart from you I have no good thing' " (16:2). Saying "You are my Lord" is a willingness to stake my present and future on God and God alone. When doubting Thomas saw the wounds of the risen Christ and was invited by Christ to place his hands on them, to attest to their genuineness, Thomas could only say, "My Lord and my God!" (Jn 20:28). These powerful words capture two distinct acts: I cry out to God. And I put my trust in God.

Third, the psalmist says, "Earnestly I seek you." These words fit perfectly with the preceding, because they give a direction to my will. I move from trust to seeking God. I now have not only a step on the path but also a direction; it is the direction of seeking God. Not only do I cry out to God and express my trust in him, but now I tell the world and my soul and God that I am seeking him. I trust him *and* I seek him. Trust may be compared to putting one's weight on a boat, while seeking is actually turning on the engine and setting out in the desired direction. I am now pointed in a direction, and I am ready for guidance.

I have spent a lot of time on the first ten words of Psalm 63 for two reasons: first, I am convinced that new worlds of understanding are sometimes contained even in small portions of a verse, and second, I feel that the three ideas of general cry, specific trust and seeking God make up the first step to regain my spiritual rhythms. The remainder of the first four verses of Psalm 63 build upon the themes already mentioned. The weary and thirsty psalmist faints for God. He, no doubt, faints also for water and rest, but the reality of his *physical* condition directs the nature of his *spiritual* quest. He remembers when he was in the sanctuary of God (v. 2), and the memory of that time is so powerful that he says, "your love is better than life" (v. 3). Surely something has happened to the psalmist in the past where the goodness of God was evident to him. Now the mere memory of it brings songs of praise to his lips. He even lifts up his hands to God. He is worshiping in the desert. Amid threatened death and ardent pursuit, where one needs to lie low, David lifts up his hands to God. "How foolish," one might say. But David trusts in God, and he is not ashamed or afraid to show it in any way.

The Yearning Fulfilled

Verses 4-8 contain some of the richest expressions of satisfaction that can be found in the Scriptures. Now that David has unreservedly put his trust in God and has resolved to seek and praise and lift up hands to God, he discovers that he is full. David does not tell us *how* the fullness will come, but he anticipates its presence. He says, "my soul will be satisfied with the richest of foods" (v. 5). He knows that he will be full, as full as after a wonderful meal. In the midst of deprivation and pursuit, David luxuriates in his fullness. Listen to his words: "with singing lips my mouth will praise you," "I sing in the shadow of your wings," "my soul clings to you" (v. 5, 7-8).

What is fascinating about this passage is that David's *objective* situation has not changed at all. He is still in the wilderness. He is still a hunted man. But, within that condition, David has learned the secret of spiritual richness. He has learned that when he fully puts his trust in God and longs for God as much as he longs for the cool refreshing stream of pure water, he finds God. He finds a deep sense of peace and acceptance. His longing has been answered by God. He was lost and now is found. He has, spiritually speaking, slain the fatted calf and feasted on it, and now he rejoices exceedingly.

There is a great lesson in David's experience for all who want to regain their spiritual rhythms. God's care really is there and is available to me irrespective of my external circumstances. Am I waiting for life to calm down before I take up my spiritual quest? Am I waiting until I have more time, until the pressures lessen, until the kids are grown, until I have enough money, until I get over this next hurdle? If that is my approach to spiritual life, I have done it backwards. David's experience teaches those who have ears to hear that God's presence can be enjoyed and luxuriated in *right now*. Right now. In the midst of the pressures and debilitating forces that eat at me, God is there. Will I seek this God now, as David did, or wait for a more "opportune" time?

God's Protection

There are two directions in the final verses of Psalm 63. On one hand, David states his confidence that his enemies will one day receive their just desserts. On the other, David, perhaps thinking of himself, declares his unreserved trust in God. He doesn't describe the mystery of God's judgment or the reasons for his belief that his enemies will fall. Such knowledge evades human understanding and is certainly "too wonderful" for us (Ps 139:6). He knows, however, that it is his task to rejoice in God. Like Joshua of old, he does not know which God others will seek, but he and his household, they will serve the Lord (Josh 24:15).

If one phrase accurately captures the way many people feel about life today, it is "out of control." I grew up with the feeling that some day, probably after I finished college and settled down, that life, too, would settle down and some kind of peaceful normalcy would result. But that simply is not true for many. Better said, that has not yet been my experience; I feel I need to rush. Everyone is in a hurry, and I need to be in a hurry too.

In a never-ending cycle I hurry for so many good reasons. I've got studying to do, family to take care of, work to perform, goals to reach, vacations to enjoy and new opportunities to grasp. If I rest, I feel that I'm being lazy, somehow not maximizing my time and talents. The demands on me never cease: if I am good at what I do, people ask me to do more. I don't want to let them down, so I accept. I would like to have time to settle down and let my heartbeat return to normal, but I feel I have to put that off. Someday, after the next deal is completed, after I have my degree or job or after the kids are out of the house, someday, I say, I will be able to relax and spend time on really important things—like cultivating my spiritual life. Yet I can't quite see that time. The horizon is still a bit too cloudy. I am sure that it will come, but am not sure when. So I put off the cultivation of my spiritual life. I flag in zeal. My life becomes an endless repetition of what I have to do, and I am enslaved to my cycle of existence. I lose hope.

I can break this cycle of relentless activity and despair by focusing on a psalm—this psalm. In Psalm 63 David has gone from unfocused longing to a statement of trust to focused desire. As a result of his focused desire on God, he finds, perhaps even to his surprise, that he is filled. His life is now overflowing with the experience of God's goodness. He experiences God's goodness in the desert, while enemies are storming the gates of his life. He does not rest,

however, in the wonder of the experience of God's goodness. He presses on
to resolution of the problem. The enemies will come to naught, and he will
continue to rejoice in God. By the end of the psalm David is stating his
confidence that there is a loving, just and active God who not only hears him,
but is worthy of David's trust and complete confidence. That is the starting
point for us in our spiritual life. Learn to long for God. Don't wait until
everything in life is "under control." Say to God right now, "O God, you are
my God, earnestly I seek you."

Prayer

*You know all my longings, dear God. My desires are not hidden from you. You know
how my longings both give me strength and destroy my rhythms. Be present with me
in my longings. Be present with me in body and soul. Be present with me in the
sanctuary and on my bed. Direct my yearnings in good and helpful channels. Satisfy
me as I seek to use my longings and energy for you. Through Jesus Christ our Lord,
Amen.*

TWO

◊

PSALMS 42—43

THIRSTING FOR GOD

For the director of music. A maskil of the Sons of Korah

[1]*As the deer pants for streams of water,*
  so my soul pants for you, O God.
[2]*My soul thirsts for God, for the living God.*
  When can I go and meet with God?
[3]*My tears have been my food*
  day and night,
while men say to me all day long,
  "Where is your God?"
[4]*These things I remember*
  as I pour out my soul:
how I used to go with the multitude,
  leading the procession to the house of God,
with shouts of joy and thanksgiving
  among the festive throng.

⁵Why are you downcast, O my soul?
   Why so disturbed within me?
Put your hope in God,
   for I will yet praise him,
   my Savior and my God.
⁶My soul is downcast within me;
   therefore I will remember you
from the land of the Jordan,
   the heights of Hermon—from Mount Mizar.
⁷Deep calls to deep
   in the roar of your waterfalls;
all your waves and breakers
   have swept over me.
⁸By day the LORD directs his love,
   at night his song is with me—
   a prayer to the God of my life.
⁹I say to God my Rock,
   "Why have you forgotten me?
Why must I go about mourning,
   oppressed by the enemy?"
¹⁰My bones suffer mortal agony
   as my foes taunt me,
saying to me all day long,
   "Where is your God?"
¹¹Why are you downcast, O my soul?
   Why so disturbed within me?
Put your hope in God,
   for I will yet praise him,
   my Savior and my God.

             *   *   *

¹Vindicate me, O God,
   and plead my cause against an ungodly nation;
   rescue me from deceitful and wicked men.
²You are God my stronghold.
   Why have you rejected me?
Why must I go about mourning,

oppressed by the enemy?
³Send forth your light and your truth,
   let them guide me;
let them bring me to your holy mountain,
   to the place where you dwell.
⁴Then will I go to the altar of God,
   to God, my joy and my delight.
I will praise you with the harp,
   O God, my God.
⁵Why are you downcast, O my soul?
   Why so disturbed within me?
Put your hope in God,
   for I will yet praise him,
   my Savior and my God.

*S*t. Augustine, a church father of the fourth and fifth centuries, wrote a great deal about faith. He wrote so much that one authority said that if anyone claims to have read all of Augustine, that person is a liar. Perhaps the most popular of his many writings is his *Confessions*, written in A.D. 398 after he had been consecrated bishop of Hippo in North Africa. He wrote the *Confessions* to tell his congregation, and the larger world, how he had come to faith in Christ and to reflect on why it had taken him so long to make a decision for Christ when the claims of the gospel were so evidently true. In one passage, when reflecting on this problem, Augustine combines his sense of wonder, longing and inquisitiveness into a hymn of praise:

I have learned to love you late, Beauty at once so ancient and so new! I have learned to love you late! You were within me, and I was in the world outside myself. I searched for you outside myself and, disfigured as I was, I fell upon the lovely things of your creation. You were with me, but I was not with you. . . . You called me; you cried aloud to me; you broke my barrier of deafness. You shone upon me; your radiance enveloped me; you put my blindness to flight. You shed your fragrance about me; I drew breath and now I gasp for your sweet odor. I tasted you, and now I hunger and thirst for you. You touched me, and I am inflamed with love of your peace. (10. 27)

Augustine was a man who never lost his sense of longing for God. His pastoral concern, theological polemics, devotional writings, sermons and commentaries and hundreds of letters are all rooted in a soul that panted for God like the deer that pants for the cool refreshing mountain streams. Augustine restlessly sought God and sought to find his rest in God. At the center of his being was the heart always burning, the mind always yearning, the total person always thirsting for God. He was a man who fully wanted to engage all his senses in his search for God. Note how the quotation draws on sound, sight, smell, taste and touch. All the senses are engaged, preoccupied, touched in the search for God and in God's search for us.

As we continue our reflections on longing for God, we can use Augustine as a model and stimulus. Augustine, in his youth, had longed deeply for things other than God—for sexual pleasure, for career success, for recognition in the larger world—but his sense of fulfillment in finding God is captured by his personal confession, made during his forties, "You have made us for Yourself, O God, and our hearts are restless until they find their rest in You" (1.1). May our hearts and minds be united and focused on the living God! May we fully use our past to aid us in our yearning for God in the present! In this spirit I invite you to continue our study of longing for God in Psalms 42—43.

Thirsting

It is striking how often in Scripture the experience of thirst and the quenching of thirst by clear, flowing water is related to our search for God. After a fire has devoured the open pastures, the prophet Joel notices how the wildlife behaves. "Even the wild animals pant for you; the streams of water have dried up" (Joel 1:20). Searching for water, searching for God. God is called the "spring of living water" (Jer 2:13). It is from God's throne that the "river of the water of life" flows (Rev 22:1). We, too, if we trust in Christ, are able to mingle our water with the divine water, for Jesus said, "If anyone is thirsty, let him come to me and drink. Whoever believes in me, as the Scripture has said, streams of living water will flow from within him" (Jn 7:37-38). Water and God are both life giving. Without them we dry up and die. Daily we need to come to the flowing stream, the river of life, to slake our thirst and refresh our lives. The deer pants for "streams of water," or, as other translations have it, "flowing streams." The deer and we long for the living, fresh, clear water of God and not the polluted, clogged waterways that are all around us. Oh God, we pray, refresh us with your clear and sparkling water that we may be filled with your goodness!

Tears of Nostalgia

Mention of water and thirsting for a quenching draught in verses 1-2 leads the psalmist to think about another kind of water—his tears. Though he longs for the limpid and refreshing river, he only can taste the salty streams of tears that course down his cheeks. He weeps because people around him are mocking him, asking him where his God is. "If your God is so great," they say, "why is your life so miserable?" The psalmist knows that they have a point; it is the same question he has: "If God is so good, and if I am an earnest believer in God, why is my life so miserable?" To find an answer the psalmist searches his *past*. He ransacks his memory much like we might rummage through an old trunk, our old high-school annuals, or papers or correspondences we have saved. He is not searching his past to write a history of his life; he is trying desperately to discover how his life went awry, how it was that he who once led a confident, faithful life in the community of believers now lives so painfully and so alone. How did the web become tangled? How did the skein of his life become so twisted? Can it ever be straightened out?

The psalmist, therefore, urges us to explore our past and to listen to our lives. Many of us were brought up in religious contexts that deemphasized personal feelings and that placed little emphasis on how past personal experience shapes our understanding of the gospel. The psalmist will have none of this. He listens to his past, even if there are only faint echoes, to see what it tells him about himself as he longs for God. He encourages us to listen to our past and to see it as a *resource* in coming to an understanding of God and the gospel:

> *These things I remember*
> *as I pour out my soul:*
> *how I used to go with the multitude,*
> *leading the procession to the house of God,*
> *with shouts of joy and thanksgiving*
> *among the festive throng. (v. 4)*

He, who is now alone, remembers the times of community. He, who is now sad, remembers transforming joy. He, who is now despondent and on the defensive, remembers when he happily led in a movement. Sometimes the vast caverns of our memory only enable us to recall the pain of life, but sometimes we recall, with tears of remembered joy, the times of fullness and happiness, when life fit and we had a vigorous role to play. But the pain of the present soon overtakes the joy of the past. The contrast is so strong; the vividness of the memory fades as he lingers on it. He returns to the pain of the moment. All he knows is that life at one time seemed to make sense. Now it does not. He chides his soul to hope again in God. But the problem is unresolved and the psalmist is uncertain.

Back to the Present

The memory was a short-lived joy, like a candle that flickered briefly and bravely in the windy night air before being extinguished by a blustery gust. So the psalmist looks at his *present situation*. He is far away from Jerusalem—the place of the temple and the visible presence of God. He is at the heights of Hermon, a towering peak in southern Lebanon. The Jordan River finds its source in the neighborhood of Hermon and, as it rushes down from mountain heights, it thunders and crashes. It is this experience of hearing the tumbling waters cascade down the mountain that lies behind verses 6-10. He hears the thundering waters below: "deep calls to deep in the roar of your waterfalls." He likens the crash of the waters to the tumultuous discord of his life: "all your waves and breakers have swept over me" (v. 7). That is, the crushing blows of the waters on the rocks below are like the crushing blows of the waves of God against him.

Instead of seeing the cascading waters as a testimony of God's awesome power or nature's controlled fury, he sees them as a physical picture of how he is being pummeled by life or, in the last analysis, pummeled by God. The waters hurtle against the rock. They explode in a fury of foam and froth, a splattering of spray and spume. "Oh God," he cries, "I'm being beaten, crushed, pummeled, drilled, blasted by these impersonal forces. They are churning out of control around me. I'm at their mercy. Why don't you enter and save? Why do the enemies keep oppressing me? Why must my tears be my food day and night? Why do I feel as if each day I am beat up by forces that are far stronger than I?"

The past did not save the psalmist. The present isn't helping much either.

He tries to reaffirm his faith in verse 8:

> By day the LORD directs his love,
> at night his song is with me—
> a prayer to the God of my life.

Though his reaffirmation might be sincere, the truth of his confession doesn't immediately change things, for he returns to the depths in verse 9. It appears that God has forgotten him, left him tethered to a pole amid the crashing waters so that the waters can vent their uncontrollable fury on him. He has confidence that he will again praise God, but reflection on the past and the present have not made that any easier. Psalm 42 closes with an unfulfilled longing. There is plenty of water, but it is the wrong kind of water: it is either the salty stream of tears or the crashing flow of the river. In neither case can he slake his thirst. He is dying of thirst in the middle of the waters.

Bright Hope for Tomorrow

Now we see why we must consider Psalm 43 with 42. For Psalm 43 continues the language and the longing of Psalm 42, but directs it to the *future*. The psalmist has come up empty as he considers the past and the present: the one provided the temporary relief of remembered joy, but that joy disappeared like a wisp of smoke; the other provided only an occasion for reflection on the degree of current distress. The psalmist doesn't, however, give up. He is like a person groping down a long, dark hallway, trying each door to see if, on the other side, there is safety and comfort. The doors marked "past" and "present" did not yield this comfort. Maybe he can look to the future. He says,

> Send forth your light and your truth,
> let them guide me;
> let them bring me to your holy mountain,
> to the place where you dwell. (v. 3)

This is the first time in the two psalms that the psalmist has actually asked God for something! He has been so wrapped up in his own concerns, so unable to feel anything beyond the contours of his own body, that he had not even asked God for help. He was full of questions but had not one supplication. Now he asks. His asking quickly leads him to action. God must send forth truth and light to lead him to the temple. Then, in verse 4, the psalmist says,

> Then will I go to the altar of God,
> to God, my joy and my delight.

I will praise you with the harp,
    O God, my God.
He knows that his thirsting for God will only be quenched when he is where
he belongs—the house of God. He knows that he must, for the moment, give
up brooding on the past, relinquish the beaten and battered feelings from the
present, and rush with speed and determination to God. He doesn't think for
a moment that the past is fully over and done or that the dragons of the present
will never again lift their ugly heads; he knows that what he needs is to embrace
and be embraced in the warm confines of the house of God. So, he runs to
God, to the house of God. Like Pilgrim in *Pilgrim's Progress* who, upon hearing
the good news of the gospel from Evangelist, plugs his ears against all contrary
words and runs headlong toward the wicket gate, shouting "Life, life, eternal
life!" so our psalmist knows that he must resist the voices that continue to dog
him about the past and present. He rushes to the altar of God, his great delight.
All is not "dealt with" fully. But he will be in the place where hope returns,
where sense is made of the past, and where an abundant stream of crystal-clear,
limpid water flows, from which he can drink deeply until he wants no more.

Prayer
*Our sovereign God, I yearn for you. Sometimes my life is so dry, dusty and deserted
that I feel I have no hope. I long for the cool, refreshing streams of your goodness,
but often I am overwhelmed by life. The past binds me. The present immobilizes me.
The future frightens me. I feel so far away from the center of life, so removed from
the unifying center of my life. I feel as if I have been crushed by life, and to that the
prospects for good change are not very hopeful. O God of my salvation, reach out
to me as I tell you my longing and my distress. Help me not to be consumed by my
past or destroyed by my present. Bring me to your special place, where you are, and
give me strength to march to your altar and sing your praises. Restore that vital center
to my existence as I thirst for you. Through Jesus Christ our Lord, Amen.*

THREE

02-08-96

◊

PSALM 84

———

HOME

For the director of music. According to gittith.
Of the Sons of Korah. A psalm.

¹How lovely is your dwelling place,
  O LORD Almighty!
²My soul yearns, even faints,
  for the courts of the LORD;
my heart and my flesh cry out
  for the living God.
³Even the sparrow has found a home,
  and the swallow a nest for herself,
where she may have her young—
  a place near your altar,
  O LORD Almighty, my King and my God.
⁴Blessed are those who dwell in your house;
  they are ever praising you.

> *⁵Blessed are those whose strength is in you,*
> *who have set their hearts on pilgrimage.*
> *⁶As they pass through the Valley of Baca,*
> *they make it a place of springs;*
> *the autumn rains also cover it with pools.*
> *⁷They go from strength to strength,*
> *till each appears before God in Zion.*
> *⁸Hear my prayer, O LORD God Almighty;*
> *listen to me, O God of Jacob.*
> *⁹Look upon our shield, O God;*
> *look with favor on your anointed one.*
> *¹⁰Better is one day in your courts*
> *than a thousand elsewhere;*
> *I would rather be a doorkeeper in the house of my God*
> *than dwell in the tents of the wicked.*
> *¹¹For the LORD God is a sun and shield;*
> *the LORD bestows favor and honor;*
> *no good thing does he withhold*
> *from those whose walk is blameless.*
> *¹²O LORD Almighty,*
> *blessed is the man who trusts in you.*

*P*salm 84 is an exuberant psalm. It pulsates with the joy of one who has come home after a long absence and a difficult return journey. Once the author has returned home to the temple of God he never wants to leave again. Psalm 84 links the powerful themes of faith and home.

Author-minister Frederick Buechner also has combined these themes by describing faith as a certain kind of homesickness. Taking his cue from Hebrews 11, where the great heroes of faith are described in their search for a homeland, Buechner sees the modern dynamic of faith as a longing for home, an inclination or inner thirst for what is not yet in hand but is vigorously desired. In this life we only catch glimpses of our true home, the kingdom of

God. Psalm 84 is a psalm that gives us a glimpse of this kingdom and puts our longing into words for us.

The words of Psalm 84 are memorable for several reasons. First, they *complete and carry forward* the hopes of Psalms 42—43. In Psalms 42—43 there was a *longing* for home; in Psalm 84 the author *is* at home. In Psalms 42—43 the author contemplated the past with a downcast spirit; in Psalm 84 the past journey is remembered with joy and praise. In Psalms 42—43 the present time brings affliction; in Psalm 84 the present time brings unmeasured delight.

Second, the words are very *visual*. We see the temple as the author sees it. We see the sparrows and swallows that make their nests there. We see, in our mind's eye, the door at which the author would rather sit than dwell in the tents of the wicked. God, for the psalmist, is a sun and a shield, a light to guide and a protector. All of us who have a need to see something to believe it should take courage through this psalm, for Psalm 84 forever affirms the centrality of visual learners for the kingdom of God. It is almost as if Psalm 84 were written for us and our visually oriented society.

Third, the words greatly *expand our understanding* of God. Usually each psalm will have one or two titles or names for God. In Psalm 84, however, the divine names pile up with grandeur. We have the Lord Almighty (v. 1), which is the name used to describe God to Abram in Genesis 17. There is "the LORD" (v. 2) and the living God (v. 2). Then we have the Lord Almighty again in verse 3. Lest we think all these titles mean that God is a distant God, the psalmist quickly adds, "my King and my God" (v. 3). We have the combination name "LORD God Almighty" and "O God of Jacob" in verse 8. The God of Jacob was the one who transformed Jacob into Israel through the night wrestling match at the Jabbok River (Gen 32). Thus, the names for God in this psalm capture the might and immediacy of God. We see God's might and sense God's closeness through the names the psalmist uses here.

Different titles for God indicate different aspects of his character. They also show that the psalmist's God cannot simply be captured in one name. His God is too big, too glorious to have one epithet suffice. May we seek to capture some of God's greatness and the psalmist's joy as we hear this psalm and try to make it our own.

The Glory of the House

The temple of God in Jerusalem is like a magnet that draws the psalmist to it and gives him true joy. When he says, in verse 1, "How lovely is your dwelling place, O LORD Almighty," he places emphasis on the word *lovely*. At first we might be surprised by the word, because the Jewish temple in Jerusalem was neither as ornate nor as large as an Egyptian pyramid or a Greek temple. It did not have the majestic symmetry of the Parthenon or the commanding presence of the pyramids along the Nile. The tides of history destroyed the Jewish temple, while some of the other ancient temples still stand. Yet the temple was lovely because of its meaning; it was the visible reminder that God dwells among his people. The temple was lovely because the God who inhabited it and directed the life of his people was lovely. Its loveliness may be partially ascribed to its architectural splendor, but the greater loveliness of the temple was the splendor of the God to whom it pointed.

The fact that the temple could be so designated and could be the focus of so much spiritual longing shows that visual imagery and sacred spaces are affirmed by the God of Israel. We are physical beings. Visible, tangible things take on special meaning for us. John Calvin taught that God gave us the sacraments of the Lord's Supper and baptism precisely because we are *sensual* beings, people who receive truth through physical objects. Places, also, can capture and communicate deep meaning for us. What are our sacred places? What are the special physical things that help communicate the presence of God? For the psalmist it was the temple, the goal of his journey, that was the very presence of God for him.

He longed for the temple when he was away. Even now, as he gazes upon it, his heart and soul still yearn for the temple and for God. To receive God is to want more of God; to gaze on God, figuratively speaking, is to want to see yet more of him. A glance does not suffice. The psalmist yearns and longs for God, for his true home, for the one who alone can bring together all the fragmented parts of existence and make them one.

As he is gazing, transfixed, at the temple, he notices some birds:

Even the sparrow has found a home,
   and the swallow a nest for herself,
 where she may have her young—
   a place near your altar. (v. 3)

Apparently, they had built their nests in the sacred precincts. The psalmist's reaction is remarkable. Instead of calling for the local animal-control people to rid the holy place of these birds, he sees their presence as an indication of

the providence of God. The same God who draws us willingly also draws the
lesser creatures to himself. The temple has an alluring and attractive capacity
to lead all of creation to it. We come willingly and the birds come instinctively,
and each gives testimony to God as the true home of all creation. What glory
and mystery the house of God possesses! Let us go to God with no delay, to
find him where he may be found, in his son Jesus Christ, and let us celebrate
that place as our true home.

The Joy of the Journey

While the author is enjoying the delights of the house of God, he thinks of
other compatriots who are making the pilgrimage to Jerusalem. Rather than
hearing the distant thunder of the waters and feeling pummeled by the deeps,
as in Psalm 42, the author now sees their trek to God's house as a joyful
journey. From the perspective of home, the journey is pleasant. This section
begins and ends with references to strength:

Blessed are those whose strength is in you. (v. 5)

They go from strength to strength. (v. 7)

Those who are on the journey to God have found their true strength; they have
captured their living rhythms; they enjoy a spiritual equilibrium.

The psalmist imagines the pilgrims going through the Valley of Baca and
rising to the mountains around Jerusalem. Normally, as people climb from the
valley to the mountain, they become tired. But here, for those who have set
their hearts on pilgrimage and are anticipating with joy their arrival at the house
of God, they go from strength to strength. As they expend more energy, they
become stronger.

We soar if our hope is in God or, in the words of Psalm 84, if we have set
our heart on pilgrimage. Let us ask God for an undivided heart—a heart that
longs to find joy on the journey, that gains strength even as we use up our
energy, that rises to new heights through yearning for God.

There is another powerful image in this section. Verse 6 says:

As they pass through the Valley of Baca,

they make it a place of springs.

The word baca is the Hebrew word for "tears" or "weeping," and some translations have "they pass through the valley of tears." This suggests two things.
First, the road to Jerusalem, the place of God, our true home, passes through
a valley of tears. Tears accompany the longing heart as it moves toward God.

Yearning for God, for peace, for harmony and unity, for restored rhythms, for understanding and love, is often accompanied by tears. Sometimes they are tears of sorrow and pain, but often the tears of those who long for God are tears of cleansing, healing or joy. Tears can have a wonderfully cathartic effect on the soul of one longing for God. Tears represent our most fervent desire to be at one with God and the world. Tears can bring an urgent release to us who are so clogged up by the pressures of the world. I go through the valley of tears in my journey of joy. I, too, weep there. In my tears I find myself and my God.

Second, as they pass through the Valley of Tears, "they make it a place of springs." As I am on my journey to God, and as I weep in my longing to be nearer to God and to be like God, others are nourished by my tears. The tears fall from my eyes, but when they hit the ground they well up as life-giving springs. The dry lands turn into fruitful lands through my tears. Through my longing the many will be watered. I need not fear my tears. I need not struggle to hide my tears and my heartfelt yearning for God; for my yearning will have a wonderfully catalytic effect on others. Their lives will be refreshed and encouraged; my presence and tears can turn the weeping valley into the fruitful valley.

The Delight of the Presence
But there simply is no place like home. After remembering the joy of the journey, the psalmist loses himself in his delight at the presence of God. His spirit is captured perfectly by verse 10:

Better is one day in your courts
    than a thousand elsewhere.

We sometimes say that a picture is worth a thousand words, and we mean by this that one visual image can carry as much meaning as a thousand words. So the psalmist is saying that one day in God's good favor carries as much meaning for him as three years outside of God's favor. When I yearn for God and come into God's presence, my perspective on time is altered. I don't measure life so much by the hours that pass as by its intimacy with God. Time is now a qualitative, and not simply a quantitative, measurement. I become lost in wonder, love and praise as I am in the presence of God. I find God to be my sun and my shield—the light on my path and my protector forever. I have known God as the "LORD Almighty," but now I also know him as "my King and my

God" (v. 3). I celebrate the fact that the one who is king of the universe has now been crowned king in my heart. My longing for God is rewarded with God's good presence.

That precious presence of God is available to all today. It starts with our willingness to long and to yearn and to direct our hearts and steps to the presence of God. It ends with enjoyment of God's presence and special intimacy with God that only his beloved can know. As we continue our meditations through distress, trust and praise, we will never be far away from longing. The quality of our longing will be the quality of our journey. Will you join with us in placing your whole trust in God, to yearn for him and his will as much as you would yearn for water in a desert land? God is faithful and will honor the honest desires of the longing heart.

Prayer
O God, you know my heart, thoughts and secrets. You know my failures, but you also know my desires. May my heart be set on pilgrimage to you. May I long for your presence and enjoy closeness with you all the days of my life. Through Jesus Christ our Lord, Amen.

PART TWO

◇

LIVING
WITH
DISTRESS

◇

FOUR *02-15-96*

◇

PSALM 102

ALONE

*A prayer of an afflicted man. When he is faint and pours out his
lament before the LORD.*

[1]Hear my prayer, O LORD;
  let my cry for help come to you.
[2]Do not hide your face from me
  when I am in distress.
Turn your ear to me;
  when I call, answer me quickly.

[3]For my days vanish like smoke;
  my bones burn like glowing embers.
[4]My heart is blighted and withered like grass;
  I forget to eat my food.
[5]Because of my loud groaning
  I am reduced to skin and bones.

⁶I am like a desert owl,
  like an owl among the ruins.
⁷I lie awake; I have become
  like a bird alone on a roof.
⁸All day long my enemies taunt me;
  those who rail against me use my name as a curse.
⁹For I eat ashes as my food
  and mingle my drink with tears
¹⁰because of your great wrath,
  for you have taken me up and thrown me aside.
¹¹My days are like the evening shadow;
  I wither away like grass.

*P*salm 102 is the first of nine psalms of lament or distress that we will study. We start our study of the psalms of distress by looking at the feeling of being alone or being abandoned by God. On each of the eight following days we will study a different aspect of distress. Distress is a very real part of our individual and corporate existence. The fact that there are more psalms of lament than psalms of praise in the Bible suggests that the Scriptures recognize how deeply the pain of life is etched on the hearts and lives of the people of God. Distress should not be glamorized or ignored; it should be given its due as a part of the varied rhythms of life which we experience in this world.

Psalm 102 speaks of the distress of loneliness. We can easily identify with the feeling of loneliness or abandonment of Psalm 102 because so often or so unexpectedly we lose people we have loved and needed for such a long time. The partings are painful; the loneliness that follows is almost unbearable. I, Glandion, remember a man, thirty-eight years old, at a conference who shared how lonely he has felt since he lost his wife to cancer. He is an accomplished person, a leader in his field and a dedicated Christian. He has all the material resources he needs. But a gaping hole now exists in his life. It is as if he has undergone major surgery and a vital organ has been removed. He feels distant from people and from himself, aimless and adrift in life.

I see a disheveled man get up to speak at a funeral. He is one of dozens of people present who remember the passing of a friend. This friend had helped hundreds of people over several years get off drugs and rebuild their lives. Now he is gone. The man who speaks is a hardened man, hardened to the ways of the street, the bruises of life, the cold, the poverty, the grinding monotony of his existence. Yet he weeps. The tears stream down his cheeks as he speaks. He doesn't know if he can make it, if he can continue to be drug-free now that his friend is gone. He feels he is alone and fighting a huge monster.

We do not have to lose a friend to feel lonely or abandoned. Sometimes loneliness and abandonment seem deeply embedded in our souls. I know I have always feared being left behind, being abandoned by my loved ones, being lost and never found. I wept as a child when my father had to go on an airplane, because I knew that he was going in the air and the air was close to God. Grandpa had just died, and I was told that he was going to God. In my childlike way I felt that if my father was going in the air, he, like Grandpa, would never come back. I would miss him so much, just like I missed Grandpa. So I clung to my mother's skirts and screamed from the depths of my being. Adults stood around, confused and pitying me. I have never really lost that fear of being abandoned. I am afraid, in the core of my being, that people, that life, that God may have abandoned me, and that the grave will be the only place where blessed peace will finally reign in my life.

So we are alone with our thoughts. We need someone outside of ourselves to hear us. We, like Job, must call to the one we fear may abandon us. Psalm 102 helps us express our loneliness and fears. It is called a psalm of lament, "a prayer of an afflicted man. When he is faint and pours out his lament before the LORD," as the superscription to the psalm says. It captures the plight of that day and of our own day. It recognizes how widespread and pervasive are our experiences and feelings of loneliness, rejection and abandonment.

I will discuss only the distress in verses 1-11 of Psalm 102. Though in some contexts an exposition of the entire psalm would be helpful, I feel at this juncture in our study that it is more important to grasp the rhythms and vocabulary of distress in this psalm than to follow the entire range of the author's thought. Though the author will eventually come out of his distress and answer his own devastation, now is the time to understand his (and our) lament.

Calling on God

The psalmist begins with a plea for God to hear:

Hear my prayer, O LORD;
  let my cry for help come to you.
It is a simple and straightforward request; it is a request for God to listen. Often when I start to pray, I feel as if my words are spoken into the tearing wind or that they disappear and die as soon as they leave my lips. Sometimes I don't even consider whether God is listening. I know my words are frail and my frame is feeble. I know my heart is fickle. I often feel that God has better things to do than to listen to me.

Before prayer becomes an effective instrument of spiritual strength for us, we need to have confidence that God hears us. Our confidence that God hears us is built upon our willingness to say, again and again, until we know that God hears us, "Hear my prayer, O LORD." Are we confident that God hears us? If so, we are ready for the next section. If not, we need to say the phrase again, perhaps with accent on different words, until we feel, deep within our being, that God will hear us. "*Hear* my prayer. Hear *my* prayer. Hear my *prayer*. Hear my prayer, O *Lord.*" Then, finally, "*Hear my prayer, O Lord.*"

The Depths of Anguish
Verses 3-11 describe what the psalmist wants God to hear. It is one of the most heart-rending passages of Scripture, for in it the author describes his weariness, loneliness, illness and feelings of worthlessness.

Three specific points or "hurts" call for comment. First, the author feels as if his life is slipping away from him.

For my days vanish like smoke;
  my bones burn like glowing embers.
My heart is blighted and withered like grass. (vv. 3-4)

My days are like the evening shadow;
  I wither away like grass. (v. 11)

These words are the first and last of this complaint section. It is as if his other complaints are sandwiched by his feelings of exhaustion and his knowledge of the impermanence of life. He is in "the midst of [his] days" (v. 24), yet his life is ebbing away, like the tide that returns to the sea. Two images stress how imperceptibly life fades away. "For my days vanish like smoke"; smoke rises and mingles with the air and gradually disappears and is gone. And "my days are like the evening shadow." The evening shadows lengthen until they become inseparable from the gradually enveloping darkness.

Even more frightening is that the fading of life leaves no trace. When the smoke is gone, there is no trace of it; when darkness has come, there is no more shadow. Perhaps the middle-aged psalmist is so distraught because he feels that were he to die now, he would disappear without a trace, without being missed, without the sense of bequeathing anything of permanence to the world. He is haunted by the fear of an unimportant, irrelevant life, of effort expended for no lasting or meaningful purpose.

Isn't the psalmist's anguish our secret anguish? That somehow, in the middle of our days, we will fade away and that no one will remember? Haven't we been told by the Scriptures and our preachers that if we believe and work for God, we may be able to accomplish great things for him? So aren't we terribly afraid that if our life were taken away now that it would have been lived in vain? That God might even be false to his promise? The key to a balanced rhythm of life is to share our honest fears and anger with God. The psalmist says, "For my days vanish like smoke . . . my days are like an evening shadow." Verbalize the complaint to God, the complaint that makes you feel lonely and abandoned. After all, you now have God's ear.

The second heartache is the psalmist's overwhelming loneliness. Only in verses 6 and 7 does he tell us what he actually feels like:

> I am like a desert owl,
>> like an owl among the ruins.
> I lie awake; I have become
>> like a bird alone on a roof.

Birds are supposed to flock together and fly. The psalmist feels he is alone and grounded. He is like the desert owl or the vulture soaring high above the sandy expanses, waiting for an opportunity to descend on putrid carrion. But, his life is contradictory. He is like the desert owl or vulture who flies; yet, he is like the bird in inhabited land who sits. Then, he simply says, "I lie awake" (v. 7).

The normal rhythms of nature are expressed in Psalm 3:5:

> I lie down and sleep;
>> I wake again, because the Lord sustains me.

In Psalm 102 he mentions his sleeplessness to show that he is out of rhythm with the order of nature. Nature teaches that birds should be together; nature teaches that birds should fly; nature teaches that we should lie down and sleep. But his experience is the opposite—awake when he should sleep, alone when he should be with others, grounded when he should be soaring. He is living out of sync with himself and with nature, and that seems to be his destiny. He is a man who no longer fits in the world, that same world in which he was brought up to fit. He feels like a piece to a jigsaw puzzle that by accident or, more frightening, by design, got put in the wrong puzzle box. He groans and weeps. He has no companions in his grief. He suffers alone. He sees no end in sight.

How lonely we feel. How arrhythmic our life has become. Our heartbeat may be normal, but we feel life is like a tight-fitting shoe, always rubbing us the wrong way, always reminding us that we don't fit. Why can't we learn the simplest lesson of nature, to lie down and sleep at night? Tell God your loneliness and your lack of accord with creation. "O God," we say, "amid our struggle against nature, restore to us the rhythms of nature and your rhythms!"

Finally, the psalmist feels that his life has become worthless and that he is no better than a piece of garbage:

For you have taken me up and thrown me aside. (v. 10)

Two images come out of these words. The first is that of a mighty wind or hurricane. God is like a windstorm that swoops down on the unsuspecting and blows them away. The second image comes from the perspective of the sufferer, who feels discarded, like one who has been swept away by a terrible power that has entered life. The winds that have destroyed everything are not the gentle breezes of the Spirit that renew life; they are the devastating gusts that overturn everything precious. All that we are and have is destroyed—so rapidly, so completely and, apparently, so ruthlessly!

Garbage. That's what I am. That is what I feel like, the psalmist says. I feel disposable, like a dirty diaper. I feel blown around, like flying paper that swirls with leaves, debris, dust and twigs in the windy whirlpools of life. So we follow the psalmist into the temple of his loneliness, and we find his and our aches and loneliness. We disappear like the smoke. We lie awake. We feel discarded and no longer needed. Living in our throwaway culture, we're afraid that we have (or will) become one of those items so easily replaced. We need to cry to God and offer our prayer and our loneliness and our arrhythmia to him. Sometimes there is immediate help from God. Sometimes we have to wait. And wait. And wait.

Prayer

Our eternal God, so often when I am in distress I lose all perspective of time and space. I am in a chasm or a pit and cannot see the surrounding countryside. All I see are the forbidding walls of the pit. My God, help me be genuine in recounting my distress, but help me also see farther than the limitations that I think are mine. May I not be dominated by the anguish that gnaws at me. Give me peace in the knowledge that you endure forever and that, at the right time, you will deliver me. Through Jesus Christ our Lord, Amen.

FIVE ◇ PSALM 130 ——— WAITING

02-22-96

A song of ascents.

¹Out of the depths I cry to you, O LORD;
 ²O Lord, hear my voice.
Let your ears be attentive
 to my cry for mercy.

³If you, O LORD, kept a record of sins,
 O Lord, who could stand?
⁴But with you there is forgiveness;
 therefore you are feared.

⁵I wait for the LORD, my soul waits,
 and in his word I put my hope.
⁶My soul waits for the Lord
 more than watchmen wait for the morning,
 more than watchmen wait for the morning.

> ⁷O Israel, put your hope in the LORD,
>   for with the LORD is unfailing love
>   and with him is full redemption.
> ⁸He himself will redeem Israel
>   from all their sins.

*P*salm 102 shows how deeply we feel our loneliness and abandonment. It would be nice, we think, if life weren't so complex, if, for example, it worked out like in the parable of the prodigal son. He, the prodigal, was alone and abandoned, in the pigsty of a far-off land, eating the pods on which the hogs fed. He got up and went home, and the embracing arms of a loving father were waiting for him. His loneliness was quickly reversed. Would that life were always that way for us. Just pick yourself up and run home, and a huge steak dinner is waiting!

Even though we welcome the truth of this most memorable parable of Jesus, we realize that life may not always work out that simply, quickly and positively. Most of us are convinced that life *seldom* works out so neatly. We believe in the grace of God, and in God's ability to reverse the upheaval of life almost immediately. But we feel that God generally doesn't work that way. Some of us are secretly convinced that the "Hold" button on the phone was really invented by a theologian who wanted to teach, by a silent but powerful lesson, that for much of our life we seem to be "on hold." Waiting.

But there are a variety of ways to wait. One can wait calmly, knowing that the train will arrive in a few minutes. One can wait with great joy and barely suppressed expectation for the birthday or Christmas that is sure to come. The waiting that is envisioned in Psalm 130 is different from these. It is like the waiting of a family in the hospital for news that a loved one has emerged safely from dangerous surgery. While the family waits, every movement is a bit edgy; nervous conversation alternates with painful silence; concentration on anything other than the loved one's well-being is impossible. One goes to the restaurant or restroom but rushes back, when one really doesn't need to rush. It is almost as if we cannot permit ourselves too much comfort when we know that our loved one is experiencing so much discomfort.

The waiting of Psalm 130 is like the waiting of most people in South Africa, black as well as white, for the ending of apartheid. Apartheid is that huge system of "apartness," mammoth in its grasp, dehumanizing in its every expression, withering in its effect on both the oppressor and oppressed. The system shall end, its end has already been proclaimed many times, but the longing for its full demolition is yet unrealized.

Psalm 130 is a psalm of waiting—urgent, hopeful waiting. It is the waiting of a distressed person who calls to God from the depths of life with the hope that he will hear and deliver. It starts in the depths and ends with confidence. The psalm is easy to memorize, and, once memorized, it can serve as an effective instrument for us, wherever we are, to calm our turbulent souls and nourish us in the middle of our waiting. Let us bring this psalm into the marrow of our being by repeated reading and praying of it, especially while we are waiting for God's clear direction in our lives.

Calling from the Depths
The psalm opens with a cry to God from the depths:
> Out of the depths I cry to you, O LORD;
> O Lord, hear my voice.

We are never told how the psalmist got to the depths. He simply is there, and he wants to get out. The image behind the word *depths* is that of being fully submerged in water. He is, as we would say, sunk or at rock bottom. We, too, have our depths. We sometimes feel we are bumping along the bottom of the ocean, with our only companions those slithery and grotesque fish that cannot live with light.

I have my depths. I have the depths of *brokenness*. I would like to be healthy and sane and full of energy and vigor, but all I can sometimes feel is the broken pieces of my life. Relationships have been shattered, trust has been broken, abuse has been suffered, anger has been expressed. Time and again, the brokenness of my life comes back to haunt me. I can be living just fine, and all of a sudden I remember past pain and sink back to the depths of life. Positions of trust in significant organizations and an ample bank account are no insurance against brokenness. I may have an outwardly happy family life and even a large circle of friends, but the stabs of my past threaten to pull out my guts. I feel sometimes as if I have been so utterly, irrevocably shattered by the past that the pieces of my life can never be put back together. My only retreat is to return to the depths—of brokenness, anger, lust and pain.

I also have the depths of *searching*. I search because I do not understand. Life is so complex, and I easily lose my way. I search for honesty because I often feel nothing but lies around me. I search for a moral center to my life. I search for love and acceptance and am sometimes tempted to search for it in the wrong places. I search desperately for an ear to hear my complaint; not just its words or its syllables, but the heart of it. I search for someone to show me how I got where I am and why the terror of the recurrent dream, the irrationality of the predictable action, or the return of the unnamed fear continues to dominate my life.

In these situations the psalmist and we know that we can, if we want, choose to rot in the depths. But he decided that he had to call to God from them. So he says, "Out of the depths I cry to you, O LORD; O Lord, hear my voice."

He says "I cry to you, O LORD" because he wants to be fully exposed to God. He is saying, "O God, I am revealing myself fully to you. I call from the depths, and I desire to be unburdened of my trouble." He wants God's truth, God's interpretation, God's constancy to attend to him in his depths. He knows instinctively that his health comes from God alone. Only God can restore his life and bring back the helpful rhythms of rest and action, work and worship, solitude and community.

Note what he *doesn't* say to God. He *doesn't* say, "hear my words" or "pay attention to the particulars of my distress" or "make sure you catch the specific order of my needs." Rather, the psalmist just wants God to hear his voice. When he says "O Lord, hear my voice," he desires God to hear the deep mood or stress points of his soul. He wants God to hear the inner torment expressed in his voice. "Not my words, but my voice" is the sentiment of the psalmist.

The first verse of Psalm 130, like the first verse of Psalm 63, gives us deep and practical guidance in our distress. It tells us that the depths are the place to call on God. Are you in your depths? Call to God from there. Don't wait until life clears up, until the kids are out of the house, until the current project is finished, until you achieve greater financial stability or until you can see your way clear from the present difficulty. Call to God from the depths right now. All we need do is say, "O Lord, hear my voice." We need not have figured out our problem. We may not even know what it is that gives us vague unease or tremendous discomfort. But that isn't important. All we need is a voice. All we need is the ability to groan. All we need is to be able to sigh deeply. The key to restoring our spiritual rhythms is to realize that the first step is so easy and so small. Call to God from the depths. Don't worry about the eloquence of your call. God is there to listen and is accomplished at interpreting the true meaning of our groans.

Waiting

After we call, we need to learn how to wait. It may be a while, quite a while, before we emerge from the depths. Granted, Jonah was catapulted out of the fish's belly at God's command after only three days. Even Job, that most impatient sufferer, was brought out of his distress in time for him to have his life nearly fully restored. But it may not always work that way. Christ himself went to the cross with the words of distress from Psalm 22:1 on his lips, "My God, my God, why have you forsaken me? Why are you so far from saving me, so far from the words of my groaning?" (see Mt 27:46). Sometimes we may even have to die without the sense that deliverance has fully come.

Much of our life is consumed by waiting. Another way of putting this is to say that a good deal of our life is occupied with the constant inner tension between hoping and possessing. We always seem to be waiting on the platform of "reality" for the train bound for "expectation." The quality of our waiting is the quality of our life. But how should we wait? The words from Psalm 130:5-6 help us.

I wait for the LORD, my soul waits,
    and in his word I put my hope.
My soul waits for the Lord
    more than watchmen wait for the morning,
    more than watchmen wait for the morning.

Watchmen are most tempted to sleep during the last watch of the night. After all, it is not too difficult to stay awake until midnight or a little later. But to stay alert until the day dawns is difficult. How much they long for a faint pink streak in the sky, the harbinger of the coming day. How much they yearn for the darkness to lift. How easy it is once the promise of the day is visible to wait until the day is fully come!

So we wait. But we wait with mature and reasonable hope. It is no accident that the psalmist waits for God more than watchmen wait for the morning. Morning will surely come. In the darkness of the night the sky seems as if it will never again receive the dawning brightness. But it will. So, in the rhythms of our lives we call and we wait. We call to God from the depths of our life, and sometimes we wonder if the reverberations of our voice are even reaching God's ears. We pour out our complaint to him. Then we go to bed. We wake up the next day, and the same duties confront us. We perform them well, and still call on God. We retire and rise again, and our life appears no different. The depths seem just as deep, the dark, just as impenetrable, and relief is nowhere in sight. At times we feel we are waiting for God in vain. Sometimes when we finally forget that we are waiting or lost, we discover that we are mysteriously found; the God for whom we longed is there. And we are convinced, convinced utterly, that God was there all along.

We wait alone and we wait in community. As Israel was told to hope in the Lord (v. 7), so the church waits for God's revelation. As the psalmist calls, so I call. The psalmist's call urges us to call. So call from the depths. Don't be concerned about the words. Wait as you work. You shall not wait in vain.

Prayer

Our loving God, I often feel as if I am in a bottomless pit. The storms of life force me deeper into it. I feel so alone. I feel that when I cry out, there is no one to hear. Sometimes I feel as if all my words and pleading don't even reach your ears. Help me realize that you are there in the depths with me and that even the darkness isn't dark to you. Help me to wait for your deliverance with as much eagerness as a night watchman waits for the day. Help me, in the meantime, to read the signs of your care displayed all around me. Through Jesus Christ our Lord, Amen.

SIX

◇

PSALM 39

———

REDISCOVERING GOD

For the director of music. For Jeduthun. A psalm of David.

¹I said, "I will watch my ways
    and keep my tongue from sin;
I will put a muzzle on my mouth
    as long as the wicked are in my presence."
²But when I was silent and still,
    not even saying anything good,
    my anguish increased.
³My heart grew hot within me,
    and as I meditated, the fire burned;
    then I spoke with my tongue:
⁴"Show me, O LORD, my life's end

and the number of my days;
let me know how fleeting is my life.
⁵You have made my days a mere handbreadth;
the span of my years is as nothing before you.
Each man's life is but a breath.
⁶Man is a mere phantom as he goes to and fro:
He bustles about, but only in vain;
he heaps up wealth, not knowing who will get it.
⁷"But now, Lord, what do I look for?
My hope is in you.
⁸Save me from all my transgressions;
do not make me the scorn of fools.
⁹I was silent; I would not open my mouth,
for you are the one who has done this.
¹⁰Remove your scourge from me;
I am overcome by the blow of your hand.
¹¹You rebuke and discipline men for their sin;
you consume their wealth like a moth—
each man is but a breath.
¹²"Hear my prayer, O LORD,
listen to my cry for help;
be not deaf to my weeping.
For I dwell with you as an alien,
a stranger, as all my fathers were.
¹³Look away from me, that I may rejoice again
before I depart and am no more."

*T*he first three psalms of distress we are studying (102, 130 and 39) treat the *distance* between the psalmist and God. The complaint of Psalm 102 is that God has abandoned the psalmist: "For you have taken me up and thrown me aside" (v. 10). Psalm 130 calls to God from a great distance: "Out of the depths I cry to you, O LORD" (v. 1).

Psalm 39 stresses that the gulf between God and humans is unbridgeable.

In Psalm 39 the psalmist is overwhelmed by his distance from God—his insignificance and frailty, the brief span of his life, and his sin. He feels he is not worthy of God's attention but hopes, nevertheless, to receive God's joy again.

It is a psalm of remarkable psychological depth, and we get the sense that maturation and personal growth is taking place before our eyes as we read. It is like seeing a time-lapse film of the psalmist's life, where months, maybe even years, of personal struggle are shown in a brief thirteen verses. Yet the time-lapse film shows a person who has gone from someone who thought he knew who God *was* and who *he was* to someone who knows who *he is now* as a human being. And he finds that when he discovers himself anew he encounters a different and more gracious God than he ever imagined.

The psalm's subject, then, is changing our mind about God and ourselves. We think we know who God is and who we are in God's sight. We live according to this understanding. Sometimes we go for quite a while without questioning who we are or who God is. But then something comes up. It might be a dramatic event—an illness, injury or loss. Or it may be simply that we are growing older and that we secretly rebel against the idea that someday our name will remain only on our tombstone. We see that any honest inventory we take of our lives must include a faith inventory. We find that the God of our youth, the God we perhaps made into an idol, is not the God we now need for our homeward journey. We need to change and reorient our life and our values. It is a painful process, like climbing a huge mountain. We don't know if we can do it. But we know, somehow, that we have to take the journey. Our intellectual and faith integrity requires it. Psalm 39 helps us in that journey.

Former Life

Why did the psalmist find himself in such turmoil? What resolution did he make? Most scholars believe that the psalmist had been suffering from a severe illness or bodily affliction. Verse 3 says:

My *heart grew hot within me,*
  and as I meditated, the fire burned.

During his illness he had a lot of time to think. He knew that a dominant strand in the theology of God's Word considered suffering as divine retribution for sinful human conduct. He may not have fully agreed with this theology, but it had such a strong grip on people that it was difficult to oppose. In this theology, suffering was understood as a "trial" or "test" that a person had to endure to demonstrate the genuineness of his or her faith. Thus, when one suffered, one should confess one's sins, cry to God for deliverance, wait patiently until God brought healing, and live as if one confidently expected God's deliverance.

The author of Psalm 39 had been brought up on this theology and was resolved to live according to it. It is analogous to the resolve of many Christians today to put on the "happy face" at church and work even when they are being torn up inside. The pressure to do this derives from a certain reading of the Scriptures. After all, didn't Jesus say that "I have come that they may have life, and have it to the full" (Jn 10:10)? Didn't Jesus pray that the disciples would have the full measure of his joy within them (Jn 17:13)? If we don't feel this joy or don't seem to express it through smiles and faithful affirmations, what does this say about us? How can we be strong Christians, we think, if we don't have the joy that seems so basic to Jesus' ministry? How will others ever be convinced to become Christians if our lives appear worse than theirs? So we try to reason away our sorrow, even though our sorrow is usually a much stronger debater than our reason.

The psalmist resolved not to breathe a word of his distress to others (verses 1-3). He was especially concerned to put a muzzle on his mouth when the wicked were around, lest they hear him, a believer, complaining against God and, thus, have reason to continue in their wickedness. So he said nothing. But his condition, rather than improving, got no better. His theology did not agree with his experience, and he felt he could discard neither. *God is good. I am in such pain. I have not done anything to deserve this. I must live with my anguish.* That is the essence of his pain. He felt he had to speak. But how?

Breakthrough

His words in verses 4-6 constitute his breakthrough, his reorientation, his movement to a deeper level of faith. He *could* have responded in two ways: first, he could have exploded in rage by lashing out at God. We know how rancorous and uncontrollable expressions of anger often come from Christians who have been trying to hold it in with all their power. They find, ultimately, that their anger has gotten the better of them. But this is not his response. Instead, he becomes overwhelmed by his brokenness, sadness and weakness. He has finally become fully aware of his frailty. He says to God in verses 4 and 5:

Show me, O LORD, my life's end

60 / LONGING FOR GOD

and the number of my days;
let me know how fleeting is my life.
You have made my days a mere handbreadth.

A handbreadth is four or five inches long. The psalmist finally realizes that his life is only that long. Perhaps before his affliction he thought, as many young people do, that he was indestructible, that he would live forever, that he could party all night and not feel the effects of it the next morning. But something has happened to him. He has become overwhelmed by his own nature. His illness has taught him his mortality. He sees himself as weak and frail, as evanescent as a wisp of prairie wind. He now knows more than ever that he is a person with limits.

At first he is astonished and even disappointed by this realization. If life is so brief, it must be in vain:

Man is a mere phantom as he goes to and fro:
He bustles about, but only in vain;
he heaps up wealth, not knowing who will get it. (v. 6)

At first he confuses brevity with meaninglessness. He assumes that since life is so short, it must be empty. But that is patently not true! Many things of short duration have deep meaning. The issue is not how long something lasts but what one does with the time one enjoys. Quality, rather than quantity, is the measure of the psalmist's life.

Many of us get caught in the predicament of the psalmist. We do not want to admit our mortality. We become defensive when our hair thins or our midsection thickens. We look back at the pleasures we once enjoyed with an exaggeration that will not stand up to scrutiny. We celebrate our fortieth birthday with black balloons and funny cards and letters. We don't want to lose this fight. We still want our youth. We don't want to feel we are closer to death. We fight it like a child who fights sleep to stay up to usher in the New Year. We feel if we admit that we will die somehow our purpose in living will be extinguished. We say with the teacher, "Meaningless! Meaningless! . . . Utterly meaningless" (Eccles 1:2). We are not yet fully converted.

Continuing Conversion
His breakthrough, or conversion, continues as he realizes that the shortness of life rather than bringing a sense of being cheated actually brings a deeper longing for God. How can one explain that spouses love each other more, even

though, as days go by, they have fewer and fewer years until one of them dies? How can one explain that life becomes more precious when there is less time for us to celebrate it? One of the great paradoxes of existence is that a lesser quantity can bring a greater joy.

Then, all of a sudden, the psalmist feels a terrible sense of unworthiness and fear. He knows that he is full of sin. His shortcomings are all around him. The frailty of his body shows him how weak he actually is. When he discovers his weakness, he knows that he is far from God. God is eternal and strong; he himself is transient and weak. God doesn't change. The psalmist changes daily. God does not decay. The author is wasting away. It is not just that he is weak or frail. He is also sinful. As we will see in the next chapter, the psalmist is deeply aware of his uncleanness, his guilt, his sin. He knows, as Paul teaches later, that in his flesh dwells no good thing.

It appears, then, that the psalmist's breakthrough has only brought him pain. It has taught him how brief his life was. It has shown him how sinful he was. It has stressed how far he is from the holy and righteous God. Maybe, he fears, once he has learned all these things, God will now pull the rug out from under him and kill him! It is like the lurking fear we have that says God is just waiting to snatch away from us the thing that we love most. The psalmist cannot retreat to his youth; he must face the new realities of existence. In the closing verse he does so by throwing himself on the grace of God and praying:

Look away from me, that I may rejoice again
before I depart and am no more.

He begs God not to look at his weakness and sin, which are so evident, and judge him harshly, but rather to look at him in mercy so that he can enjoy the life that is left him. The sentiment expressed is identical to that in another psalm:

Remember not the sins of my youth
and my rebellious ways;
according to your love remember me,
for you are good, O LORD. (25:7)

But as we pray for God to "remember me" or to "look away from me," we know that we have no independent ground on which to stand, no claim on God's mercy. Without God's grace we are lost. Ultimately, we will need another who can intercede for us, who can make our case for us before the Father. The psalm points us to our need for a Savior, Jesus Christ. As the New Testament teaches,

If anybody does sin, we have one who speaks to the Father in our defense—Jesus Christ, the Righteous One. (1 Jn 2:1)
As we realize our mortality, we may be tempted to see it only as something we have lost. We feel, at first, that something has been taken away. We are adrift and frustrated and even angry. Then, as our mortality sinks in on us, we see our sin and failure, our alienation from God and our brokenness, our futility and our sin. We need then to throw ourselves on the mercy of God; for we know we have nothing to offer God. But then, we find that God is there, that he will not abandon us, that he will reach out to us and grasp our desperate and quivering hand. Then, we will know the joy of being found, the surprise and pleasure that can be enjoyed in the few days we have.

Prayer
Our heavenly Father, bring me through the great transitions of life. Help me not to be so scared of them. Help me see my emptiness and mortality and your grace and your fullness. Help me embrace the life that is there, beckoning me in Christ. Through Jesus Christ our Lord, Amen.

SEVEN

◊

PSALM 51

GUILTY

For the director of music. A psalm of David. When the prophet Nathan came to him after David had committed adultery with Bathsheba.

¹Have mercy on me, O God,
*   according to your unfailing love;*
according to your great compassion
*   blot out my transgressions.*
²Wash away all my iniquity
*   and cleanse me from my sin.*

³For I know my transgressions,
*   and my sin is always before me.*
⁴Against you, you only, have I sinned
*   and done what is evil in your sight,*
so that you are proved right when you speak
*   and justified when you judge.*
⁵Surely I was sinful at birth,

sinful from the time my mother conceived me.
⁶*Surely you desire truth in the inner parts;*
   you teach me wisdom in the inmost part.

⁷*Cleanse me with hyssop, and I will be clean;*
   wash me, and I will be whiter than snow.
⁸*Let me hear joy and gladness;*
   let the bones you have crushed rejoice.
⁹*Hide your face from my sins*
   and blot out all my iniquity.

¹⁰*Create in me a pure heart, O God,*
   and renew a steadfast spirit within me.
¹¹*Do not cast me from your presence*
   or take your Holy Spirit from me.
¹²*Restore to me the joy of your salvation*
   and grant me a willing spirit, to sustain me.

¹³*Then I will teach transgressors your ways,*
   and sinners will turn back to you.
¹⁴*Save me from bloodguilt, O God,*
   the God who saves me,
   and my tongue will sing of your righteousness.
¹⁵*O Lord, open my lips,*
   and my mouth will declare your praise.
¹⁶*You do not delight in sacrifice, or I would bring it;*
   you do not take pleasure in burnt offerings.
¹⁷*The sacrifices of God are a broken spirit;*
   a broken and contrite heart,
   O God, you will not despise.

¹⁸*In your good pleasure make Zion prosper;*
   build up the walls of Jerusalem.
¹⁹*Then there will be righteous sacrifices,*
   whole burnt offerings to delight you;
   then bulls will be offered on your altar.

S

o far we have examined the feelings *of loneliness, fear, waiting and dis-tance.* Now let us turn to the *people* whom we feel are instruments of our distress. I refer to these individuals or groups as our enemies. You may feel that you have no enemies. Closer inspection reveals three enemies, whether real or perceived—the self, God and other people. While the psalmist never breaks down his categories of enemies as neatly as this, each one is there in the psalms and each presents particular problems.

We begin with Psalm 51, a psalm of confession or lament. In moving lan-guage the author confesses his sin and his longing for cleansing. The intensity of feeling comes from the psalmist's realization that *he, and he alone,* has brought this horrible predicament on himself. He has become his own worst enemy.

As Walt Kelly's character Pogo said, "We have met the enemy and he is us." My most severe critic, my most unforgiving judge, my most merciless accuser is *me.* Often I try to deflect the blame by pointing the finger at others as cause of my distress, but secretly I feel responsible for my failure. My feelings are more complex than that; I feel both a failure *and* a victim. That is, when I look at my life, I recognize how easy and proper it is to stress how I have been victimized: by parents, teachers, so-called friends and family members. I have enough feelings of victimization to justify deep depression and even, at times, retaliation.

Yet, I feel also I'm responsible for my life and that I simply cannot blame others for my predicament. I am always "available," and my family and friends are not; so I become the focus of my abuse, criticism and relentless attack. I become prosecuting attorney, judge, jury and jailor against myself. I proclaim myself guilty with gusto. I slam down the gavel in my mind and pronounce sentence. Then I punish myself, denying simple pleasures or even normally expected things because I don't *deserve* them. I lacerate myself, if not physically then certainly mentally, because I feel unworthy of love. I act unfaithfully because it doesn't matter how I act, since I'm so monumentally out of rhythm. I recognize my need to get beyond the cycle of self-accusation and punishment, but I am at a loss how to do so.

Psalm 51 is so valuable to us because it both recognizes our sense of guilt and explores how to move beyond self-accusation and into a new life with God. I invite you to consider, then, not just the words of this psalm, but the story in David's life that provoked it.

The superscription to Psalm 51 calls it "a psalm of David, when the prophet Nathan came to him after David had committed adultery with Bathsheba." It refers to a time in David's life when he had lost his rhythm and had done some terrible things that led to the unraveling of his personal and family life. The events are described in 2 Samuel 11-12 and are much more complex than the superscription to Psalm 51 indicates.

David's troubles began when his nation was at war. In the spring of the year, when kings went to war, David sent out his troops under the command of Joab. But he stayed in Jerusalem (2 Sam 11:1). He was a warrior, and he had recently led a group of Israelites in a dramatic victory against the Arameans (2 Sam 10). (He was so good when he was in his element. No one could touch him!) For some reason, however, this year he decided to stay in Jerusalem; it is not clear *why* he remained. Perhaps he had confidence in Joab. Perhaps, however, he was growing dissatisfied with the hard life of war and wanted to develop other areas of his life. We recognize this truth in our own experience.

Many of us have been working hard all of our lives, and we have never stopped to ask some basic questions about our loves, desires and motivations. We would just like to stop working so frenetically and experiment, or see what life looks like when we are not so engaged in our work. Perhaps we have gotten to the point in life where we do not want to be so one-dimensional anymore. We discover that there is more to life, that we have capacities and interests and desires that have not been nurtured as we have grown, and that we want to begin to nurture them.

Much of this may lie behind David's decision to stay home. It is enough to say that while he was home, he was looking for something to bring a greater sense of fullness to his life. Should he have been out in the battle? Maybe. That was certainly where his former success was. But now something else was driving David, a yearning not just for the adulation that came from military victory but a yearning for full acceptance and nurturing and closeness that his military successes could not bring. His earlier life patterns were no longer satisfying. His heart wanted to discover new experiences, new patterns, new excitement.

Though the Scripture is not clear on this point, it has been convincing to us that David, for all his fame and prowess at an early age, had neglected the side of him that craved emotional tenderness and intimacy. Perhaps he never had the kind of parental love he needed. After all, he was one of seven children. Neither his mother's name or person is ever mentioned in the Scripture. Even so, David showed his concern for people early in life. He played the lyre and calmed King Saul. His intimate friendship with Jonathan showed his desire for more than just military camaraderie. His anger and genuine sadness at the death of his declared enemy, King Saul, showed how deeply he loved the nation and the office of king. He was a man who felt deeply, but rarely were his expressions of tenderness reciprocated. We believe that David greatly missed the times of sweet tenderness and closeness, the "billing, cooing, panting and wooing" of love. It is interesting that when he confesses his huge sin in Psalm 51, he uses the plural of a Hebrew word in verse 1 (translated "great compassion" in our Bibles) whose singular is always translated "womb." That is, in his moment of deepest alienation and guilt, David asks God to forgive him "with womblike love." He knows that he needs that kind of tender care.

David's interest in Bathsheba, then, is not simply because he wanted to "play around." Lust and passion are, no doubt, present, but the beats of the old rhythm of his life sounded hollow to him. He felt out of place in Jerusalem. He was looking for a new rhythm, a new tune.

When we are out of rhythm or out of place, we feel weak. When we are weak, we want to do something that makes us feel strong. When we have lost our rhythms, we want to do something that enables us to regain them, to convince ourselves that we are still in control of our lives. When we lose our rhythms, we also lose the sense of our own vulnerability. David, then, had lost his rhythms and was vulnerable. He couldn't sleep. So he got up to take an evening walk around the roof of his palace. And there she was! Bathsheba was at her home bathing: she was visible and inviting.

The rest of the story really needs no lengthy exposition. Bathsheba, whose Hittite husband was off fighting King David's war, was summoned by the king. He slept with her. She became pregnant. David recalled her husband, Uriah, from the fighting to try to get him to sleep with his wife (to give no one reason to think that the baby was other than Uriah and Bathsheba's child). He did not. David got him drunk and still he refused. David then sent a note by the hand of Uriah to Joab, showing how Joab should maneuver the troops so that Uriah would be killed. When Uriah died in battle, David took Bathsheba for his wife. A child was born. It appeared that everything was taken care of.

But, of course, it wasn't. God saw David's sin. Through God's messenger, Nathan, the sin was exposed. David knew it. He was utterly devastated, not simply because his terrible conduct had been revealed, but because he saw, immediately and instinctively, the depth to which he had fallen. His rhythms were completely shattered. His life was in immediate shambles. He had no place to run, nowhere to hide. He was exposed, naked, without even a blade of grass to hide himself. He was caught and his naked frame was frozen in the glare of the divine searchlight. He was mortified.

Psalm 51 has traditionally been read as the psalm that captures David's feelings after being exposed by Nathan. It may have been written by David or by another; it may even have been written at another time. The major point, however, is that Jews and Christians have recognized that this psalm captures the essence of the human need for forgiveness.

Obsessed by Guilt

In Psalm 51 David is overwhelmed by his sin and guilt. *Overwhelmed* is perhaps too weak a term. He is obsessed with his sin, plagued by it. In Psalm 39 the psalmist bemoaned the human condition; in Psalm 51 he is utterly cast down by his specific actions as well as by the general human condition. The author of Psalm 51 has done something that made him see that he was not just *capable* of radical evil, but that he had *actually done it*. The spirit of Psalm 51 is not simply the psalmist admitting he is a sinner. Rather, he knows in the deepest recesses of his heart that he has planned, participated in, pulled off and then tried to ignore a huge series of evils in his life—adultery, deception, murder, betrayal. So great is his sin and so significant is the evil he has done that he knows he is lost. He says,

> For I know my transgressions,
> and my sin is always before me. (v. 3)

He cannot get that thought out of his mind. It is worse than a crazy tune that keeps playing over in our minds, worse than the relentless glare of the car headlights in the rearview mirror, more deafening than the pounding of a pile driver. It infects even the air that he breathes and the food that he tastes. All his senses are obsessed with the stench of his sin. He needs some kind of divine disinfectant to carry away the death that he carries within his breast. This preoccupation with his sin makes the psalmist think that his condition is inherited and not simply chosen:

Surely I was sinful at birth,
sinful from the time my mother conceived me. (v. 5)

Longing for Cleansing

The psalmist longs for cleansing, healing and a new beginning. The metaphors for purification recur in Psalm 51: "Wash me . . . cleanse me . . . cleanse me . . . wash me . . . create in me a pure heart." He feels vile and sordid. He begs God to use the most potent cleanser to restore him. He is fully conscious that his salvation is totally outside of him; if God does not help him he will be irretrievably lost. God, the one most offended, the one who set the standards, must save the one who violated them.

Now the psalmist longs for forgiveness as much as he ever longed for God. He knows he has failed himself and God. He knows he is guilty. He wants a pure heart, a new and right spirit. He wants to be plunged beneath the cleansing stream of divine love. He has been his own worse enemy. Now he needs to start over, by God's grace.

We live in an age that would like to get rid of guilt. Guilt, we are told, is not healthy; it is self-defeating and self-destructive. Lay it aside, we are advised. The psalmist knows differently. He knows not only our capacity for but our actual practice of terrible evil. We don't know ourselves until we recognize the depth of our capacity for evil and our inclination to think and perform evil. As Paul says, "I know that nothing good lives in me, that is, in my sinful nature" (Rom 7:18). We fool ourselves if we think we don't need forgiveness. We need the compassion of God to get us out of our mess and restore us to healthy rhythms. We need to be rescued from ourselves; for sometimes we are the most fearsome enemy that stalks our path.

Prayer

Forgive, O Lord, my death wishes. I wish it for others and for myself. Forgive my desire to harm others. Forgive my desire to destroy myself. Give me a glimpse of my radical evil, O Lord, but only a glimpse, lest I lose hope completely. Cover me with the arms of your eternal love. Through Jesus Christ our Lord, Amen.

EIGHT

◇

PSALM 55

ATTACKED

For the director of music. With stringed instruments. A maskil of David.

¹*Listen to my prayer, O God,*
  do not ignore my plea;
  ²*hear me and answer me.*
My thoughts trouble me and I am distraught
  ³*at the voice of the enemy,*
  at the stares of the wicked;
for they bring down suffering upon me
  and revile me in their anger.

⁴*My heart is in anguish within me;*
  the terrors of death assail me.
⁵*Fear and trembling have beset me;*
  horror has overwhelmed me.

⁶I said, "Oh, that I had the wings of a dove!
  I would fly away and be at rest—
⁷I would flee far away
  and stay in the desert;
⁸I would hurry to my place of shelter,
  far from the tempest and storm."

⁹Confuse the wicked, O Lord, confound their speech,
  for I see violence and strife in the city.
¹⁰Day and night they prowl about on its walls;
  malice and abuse are within it.
¹¹Destructive forces are at work in the city;
  threats and lies never leave its streets.

¹²If an enemy were insulting me,
  I could endure it;
if a foe were raising himself against me,
  I could hide from him.
¹³But it is you, a man like myself,
  my companion, my close friend,
¹⁴with whom I once enjoyed sweet fellowship
  as we walked with the throng at the house of God.

¹⁵Let death take my enemies by surprise;
  let them go down alive to the grave,
  for evil finds lodging among them.

¹⁶But I call to God,
  and the LORD saves me.
¹⁷Evening, morning and noon
  I cry out in distress,
  and he hears my voice.
¹⁸He ransoms me unharmed
  from the battle waged against me,
  even though many oppose me.
¹⁹God, who is enthroned forever,

> will hear them and afflict them—
> men who never change their ways
> and have no fear of God.
>
> 20My companion attacks his friends;
>   he violates his covenant.
> 21His speech is smooth as butter,
>   yet war is in his heart;
>   his words are more soothing than oil,
>   yet they are drawn swords.
>
> 22Cast your cares on the LORD
>   and he will sustain you;
>   he will never let the righteous fall.
> 23But you, O God, will bring down the wicked
>   into the pit of corruption;
> bloodthirsty and deceitful men
>   will not live out half their days.
>
> But as for me, I trust in you.

W hen the self is assailing us, as we saw in Psalm 51, we may need
to recognize and confess our guilt and ask for a new and pure heart from God.
When the enemies are people outside of ourselves, however, we react differently. We may not like everything in Psalm 55, but its spirit and its petitions
accurately reflect how hurt we feel when we are attacked and how much we
desire retaliation against those who have injured us.

Psalm 55 is full of the confusion, contradictions and primal screams of a
person who feels suddenly set upon by others. The psalmist's mind darts
quickly from one subject to another: from a plea for God to hear, to the desire
to flee, to longing for judgment on the enemies, to identification of the betrayer, to a death wish for the betrayer, back to trust in God and to desire for
punishment of the offender, and then to a final statement of trust in God. He

appears agitated and highly charged. In contrast to Psalm 39, which we argued was like a "time-lapse" film in the psalmist's life, Psalm 55 flows directly from the wounded heart onto the paper. It is like an oil pipeline that has burst, and the inky, dirty, but valuable, oil spews all over the landscape.

The author of Psalm 55 is under intense pressure—pressure that has blasted his sense of balance. He is full of agony and anxiety. The external threats of his enemies have been transmuted into his own inner turmoil, and he has become a raging cauldron of conflicting emotions. It is as if a ferocious animal has targeted him; his pain is deep and lacerating. One can almost see the scars being carved into the flesh of the psalmist as he utters this urgent cry to God.

This is not a psalm for those who feel life is a glorious, smooth-flowing river, gently wending its way through a peaceful plain. Nor is it one for those who feel that faith should be easily consistent and rationally articulated. It is best understood by those who know their own weakness and sin, who have experienced withering scorn or attack and who still would like to affirm faith. It is the cry of a wounded person who wants to be made whole again. I invite you, fellow sinner, to consider Psalm 55 with me.

Oppression

Once again, as in Psalms 102 and 130, the psalmist begins with a cry for God to hear him:

> Listen to my prayer, O God,
>> do not ignore my plea.

It is not a bad idea, even in desperate straits, to start our prayer this way. The first step in helping us regain our sense of calm and rhythm is to quietly reaffirm the existence of a good God outside of ourselves. When pressures abound, our faith world and our emotional world threaten to collapse around us, and we lose a sense that an eternal God still is there, ready to save. Praying these words can remind us that God still rules over all, and that there is more to life than the narrow walls that encircle and stifle us.

Having asked for God's ear, the psalmist is now free to utter his complaint:

> My thoughts trouble me and I am distraught
>> at the voice of the enemy,
>> at the stares of the wicked;
> for they bring down suffering upon me
>> and revile me in their anger. (vv. 2-3)

Later in the psalm he describes the betrayal by an intimate friend, but this is
not an easy subject, and it takes him several verses to lay his soul bare and
describe how betrayal feels. So he starts in the first few verses with the attacks
of unnamed foes. But, even as he describes his trouble, his anxiety and rage
increase. The personal attacks have reached to the core of his being, threatening
his identity and self-confidence.

Attacks are like that. They have a way of shocking me, unnerving me, freez-
ing me. I become immobilized for a moment and am unsure how to respond.
I am taken aback, and I feel violated. I want to cry or retaliate or escape or
ignore the attack all at the same time. The violence visited upon me becomes
internalized. My stomach churns; my breathing becomes labored; my limbs
shake; my voice quavers. I lose my balance even if I still try or manage to
project an external calm. I become a shivering mass of protoplasm.

Attacks can come at any time for almost any reason. Note two phrases the
psalmist uses: "the voice of the enemy" and "the stares of the wicked." People
frequently use voices and stares to attack us. The voices say something to this
effect: "You are no good. You are wrong. You did a bad job. You are not
qualified. You really blew it this time." It is always *you, you, you!* The voices
question our competence, intelligence, values or integrity. No matter how
smart we feel we are, how many academic degrees we have or how diligently
we do our work—the attacks come. If we are female or a member of a minority
group, the "voices" and the "stares" that come our way are often laced with
enough ambiguity so that we don't know whether we are being criticized for
our performance or our race or sex. We often feel that the bottom line around
the office is not how competent we are but whose ally we are.

When attacked, I feel a volcanic eruption within me. Molten lava gushes
down the slopes and threatens to cover every inch of my inner space with its
deadly flow. I feel the sting of attack so deeply because I fear that some of the
criticism may be justified. I often feel inadequate, stupid, slow and incapable.
I make bundles of mistakes. I laugh at jokes even if I don't "get" them, in order
not to appear to be too slow. And, underneath it all, I fear that I may be as
fraudulent as a three-dollar bill. I fear that my incompetence will be discovered
someday and that I will be fired and exposed as the incapable person that
somehow I have always thought myself to be.

When I am attacked, I don't know whom to believe anymore. I would like
to believe my "better" self, the self that has begun believing over a long period

of time that I am a person of dignity and that I have a lot to offer people. But when the attack comes, I become almost psychologically oppressed and unable to believe the truth of my better self. I have a crisis of truth. Whom do I believe? To whom do I listen? Whom do I trust? The inner cacophony of competing voices, the pounding within, may become so loud that I can't hear any voice with clarity. I say, with the apostle Paul, "What a wretched man I am! Who will rescue me from this body of death?" (Rom 7:24). As the volume grows, so does my desperation. I am overcome by primal fears. I become a tangled mess of crossed and frayed wires. I have to do something.

Escape

The psalmist faces these same feelings. He decides he has to escape. Like Dorothy in *The Wizard of Oz*, facing the angry Elmira Gulch who wants to take away poor little Toto, he too says, "I've got to get away. I've got to run away." Only, the psalmist wants to flee his troubles even more than this. He wishes he could *fly* away (verses 6-8):

> I said, "Oh, that I had the wings of a dove!
> I would fly away and be at rest—
> I would flee far away
> and stay in the desert;
> I would hurry to my place of shelter,
> far from the tempest and storm."

He cannot get away fast enough. He wants to leave it all. Now. He longs for the place of safety and shelter, where there is peace at last. Like the battered woman in our society, he must get away to a place, any place, where the enemy cannot reach. The psalmist wants his own magic city, complete with a protective moat, drawbridges and portcullises without number, thirty-foot-thick and fifty-foot-high walls, crenelated towers with armed guards every twenty feet, locked inner passageways, soundproof rooms, and finally, an inner sanctum to which no one but he has the key! He wants the quiet of the desert where the intensity of his conflicting inner sounds can gradually die down and merge with the silent but palpable rhythms of the wilderness. He desperately wants the return of a quiet balance and a calm rhythm.

Prayer, Rage and Attempts to Trust

For the rest of the psalm the author seeks this calm rhythm without ever actually reaching it. The pain of the attack is too severe, and his hopeless rage, too strong. He makes many efforts to return to a trust in God, but his mind is constantly drawn back to the violation he feels and the vengeance he seeks.

At first he only wants God to confuse the speech of the wicked (v. 9). After all, it was the *voices* of the wicked that led him to lose his center; perhaps if their tongues were confused, the confusing voices in his head would be clarified. But then, he gets to the nub of the problem. He was not simply attacked; he was betrayed by a close friend (vv. 12-14). When he reflects on this betrayal, he is once again engulfed in helpless anger. He feels like a long-married husband, much in love, whose wife asks him for a divorce. The primal sense of violation, of waste, of loss is almost too much to bear. "You, the betrayer, are taking my *life* with you when you go."

The hatred wells up and billows, like the raging clouds of a gas fire that roll and pillow up and out and crackle with intense heat. Verse 15 expresses this primal hatred:

> Let death take my enemies by surprise;
> let them go down alive to the grave,
> for evil finds lodging among them.

All masks are off; pretense is shattered. Finally, the psalmist knows what he wants. He wants his enemies dead. He gives no indication that he will arm himself for the task; he just prays to God that they may be killed. Lest we think that this just "slipped" out of his mouth and that he really didn't mean it, we have verse 23,

> But you, O God, will bring down the wicked
> into the pit of corruption;
> bloodthirsty and deceitful men
> will not live out half their days.

He wants not only to have his enemies killed; he wants, figuratively, to dishonor their corpses.

It is striking that along with these stark, primal, unrelenting expressions of woe for his enemies are his attempts to trust God. He expresses his trust in God three times:

> But I call to God,
> and the LORD saves me. (v. 16)
> Cast your cares on the LORD
> and he will sustain you;

he will never let the righteous fall. (v. 22)
But as for me, I trust in you. (v. 23)

Side by side are expressions of the most gruesome vengeance and the most simple trust in God. Within him, feelings of revenge war with feelings of quiet trust in God.

The battle rages on in the psalmist as the psalm closes. Like many of us today, he is wrestling with a dilemma, and he cannot resolve it. In the betrayal he sees the bleak reality of human failure, but he also has faith in God who will "never let the righteous fall." Both sides of the dilemma call out for immediate and complete attention.

We are left with the sense that, however beautiful the psalm may be, it is incomplete. The psalm itself longs for fulfillment, for completeness, where judgment and mercy, faith and action, attacks and trust are somehow caught up in one person. In this way, the psalm longs for Christ, in whose life and ministry the two horns of the dilemma are perfectly and harmoniously lived.

Thus the psalm points us also to Christ, the one who can unravel the tangled pattern of our lives, the one who can help us sort through the violent feelings of revenge and the feeble attempts to trust God, the one who can provide us with strength to restore our balance and harmony even when we are attacked.

Prayer

O God, my life becomes so easily shattered when I am attacked. I hate the critical and carping voices and the stares of those who would hurt me. I want to flee. I wish vengeance so easily. I lose my symmetry and balance so quickly. Restore me, I pray, to a trust that leaves the future in your hands. Through Jesus Christ our Lord, Amen.

NINE

03-21-96

◇

PSALM 44

———

REJECTED

For the director of music. Of the Sons of Korah. A maskil.

¹We have heard with our ears, O God;
  our fathers have told us
what you did in their days,
  in days long ago.
²With your hand you drove out the nations
  and planted our fathers;
you crushed the peoples
  and made our fathers flourish.
³It was not by their sword that they won the land,
  nor did their arm bring them victory;
  it was your right hand, your arm,
  and the light of your face, for you loved them.

⁴You are my King and my God,
  who decrees victories for Jacob.
⁵Through you we push back our enemies;

through your name we trample our foes.
⁶I do not trust in my bow,
  my sword does not bring me victory;
⁷but you give us victory over our enemies,
  you put our adversaries to shame.
⁸In God we make our boast all day long,
  and we will praise your name forever.

⁹But now you have rejected and humbled us;
  you no longer go out with our armies.
¹⁰You made us retreat before the enemy,
  and our adversaries have plundered us.
¹¹You gave us up to be devoured like sheep
  and have scattered us among the nations.
¹²You sold your people for a pittance,
  gaining nothing from their sale.

¹³You have made us a reproach to our neighbors,
  the scorn and derision of those around us.
¹⁴You have made us a byword among the nations;
  the peoples shake their heads at us.
¹⁵My disgrace is before me all day long,
  and my face is covered with shame
¹⁶at the taunts of those who reproach and revile me,
  because of the enemy, who is bent on revenge.

¹⁷All this happened to us,
  though we had not forgotten you
  or been false to your covenant.
¹⁸Our hearts had not turned back;
  our feet had not strayed from your path.
¹⁹But you crushed us and made us a haunt for jackals
  and covered us over with deep darkness.

²⁰If we had forgotten the name of our God
  or spread out our hands to a foreign god,

21would not God have discovered it,
    since he knows the secrets of the heart?
22Yet for your sake we face death all day long;
    we are considered as sheep to be slaughtered.

23Awake, O Lord! Why do you sleep?
    Rouse yourself! Do not reject us forever.
24Why do you hide your face
    and forget our misery and oppression?

25We are brought down to the dust;
    our bodies cling to the ground.
26Rise up and help us;
    redeem us because of your unfailing love.

A few years ago I, Bill, ran into a seminary classmate at a conference. He had always been a fun-loving, exuberant person in school, yet as we talked I detected an unspoken sadness in his words. As our conversation developed, he shared with me that he was facing an imminent divorce. He and his wife had been drifting apart for so many years that divorce seemed their only choice. They had seen counselors and had made resolutions. They had tried and tried, but they simply could not make things work. The divorce was tearing both of them apart; yet they seemed helpless to put things back together.

In this situation all my friend could think about was his youth. He mentioned the time when he was a boy, living near Philadelphia, and he remembered the endless summer evenings listening to the Phillies on the radio in the screened-in porch. He spoke of the crack of the bat, the roar of the crowd, the announcer's excited description. He remembered listening to the whole game, lying down to sleep, awakening the next morning and dashing to get the newspaper to read the box score of the game. "Life," he said to me, "was so simple then. How did it become so confusing and complicated? Why can't I return to that joyful simplicity of youth? Are the security, peace and excitement of those warm summer nights of my youth gone forever?"

The author of Psalm 44 also longs for the simplicity and clarity of faith of a former time. He wishes that God's action and love were as evident to him and his community of faith now as they appeared to be to the heroes of the past. Somehow, he feels that everything *used to be* clear long ago, but *now* everything is confusing. He longs for the time when life was uncluttered and easy to interpret, when safety, security and ready answers were available to him.

The author of Psalm 44 also had hoped that the faith of his youth would carry him through to the end of his days. However, now the psalmist wonders if his faith needs to be redefined in the current situation. The crisis of the psalm is how to keep a vital faith in God even when life, and God, are not working as we expected them to. It is about the futile attempt to live *our* faith through *someone else's* experience. It is about the process of fashioning an adult faith, a faith that wants to affirm the gracious love of God in the midst of life's crushing load and apparent rejection by God. Thus, in Psalm 44 the author seeks to recapture the rhythms of faith and life. Can my parents' God be my God? Can their faith sustain me?

In Psalm 44 the author feels that God has rejected him and the people of God. He feels rejection, yet he doesn't express his anguish with the ardent outbursts of Psalm 55 or the humbling emptiness of Psalm 51. The language of Psalm 44 is balanced, dignified and poetically formal. One doesn't have the sense of being completely undone by life, as was the author of Psalm 39. It is as if the writer here is making a formal plea in a court setting to God. "Here is the evidence from the past," he says. "Here is the evidence from the present. You, O listener (and he hopes that God is the principal listener), decide whether I have a just and noble cause." Nevertheless, there is a note of urgency in this psalm. He wants God to rise and act on his behalf. This appeal to God is no less urgent or heartfelt than that of the psalmist who waited for God, "more than watchmen wait for the morning" (Ps 130). An importunate heart palpitates under the apparently placid surface of this psalm.

Past Mercies

The problem of Psalm 44, rejection by God, is not broached until verse 9. The deeper problem of the psalm, God's continual silence, does not come up until verse 23. Yet, the psalmist prepares the ground for those huge complaints much like the farmer readies the land before planting a crop.

He starts with the history of the chosen people. In the days long ago God was active and did wonderful things. He drove out nations, planted the ancestors, gave them victory wherever they went. God did this because he loved them. The national past, as the psalmist heard it and taught it, consisted of God's activity. It is clear and glorious. It is simple and unambiguous. God acted, and we got the land. The psalmist betrays no trace of disbelief or skepticism about this narrated past; he seems to affirm it fully.

Until Today

It adds to the drama of the psalm that his same confidence in divine activity and initiative continues to the present. Note verse 4:

You are my King and my God,
    who decrees victories for Jacob.

The psalmist is saying that the story of God's past mercies is the same as this story in my own generation. The King of old is my King. The confession of verse 4 is reminiscent of Thomas's confession to Jesus after he saw the wounds in Jesus' hands and side. When Thomas saw for himself that the Lord was risen, he said, "My Lord and my God!" (Jn 20:28). The psalmist is saying that the faith of his parents is his faith, that the God of the previous generation is his God, and it is this God that he will praise forever and ever. What parent wouldn't be overjoyed! The psalmist has repeated his catechism with skill. He knows all the answers about how God is supposed to act and how God acts.

Loss and Anger

Yet, when all is said and done, life is not a catechism. All the learned answers from the past may help little in facing the onslaught of the present. The psalmist's apparently bold declarations of faith in verses 1-8 are really nothing more than a veil that conceals the real action, a curtain that must be removed to show what is, in fact, being lived. When the curtain is drawn back, we hear the problem.

But now you have rejected us and humbled us;
    you no longer go out with our armies. (v. 9)

The two little words but now are among the most powerful in Scripture. Suddenly, with one fell swoop, all the affirmations of the previous verses are called into question. These two words are like a tiny ceiling crack that may soon turn into a massive fissure, or a minuscule growth that might turn into a life-threatening tumor. "But now" is the bracing wind of the present that shakes us out of our reverence for the past. It is the child's shriek in the night that awakens us to the immediate demands of the present. "But now" terrifies us with its directness and power.

In vain does the psalmist retreat to the pieties of the past for comfort. The meaningful catechism that he recited so flawlessly in verses 1-8 is no longer on his lips. The words which were life-giving to earlier generations now sound like a hollow gong. The past has ceased to bring life to him and to his community of faith in the present. Neither his parent's past nor his own past sheds light on the present. Thus, he has lost his two sources of rhythm and structure: God and history. Instead of honor there is disgrace, instead of laughter there are laments, instead of pride there is shame. He has lost his sure and steady sense of an order or stabilizing force in life.

To put things differently, the psalmist is angry. He continues to address God in the second person in verses 9-14, but every blessing of God narrated in verses 1-8 is now negated. "You drove out the nations" (v. 2). Now, however, "you made us retreat before the enemy" (v. 10). Then, "you crushed the peoples" (v. 2). Now, "you gave us up to be devoured like sheep" (v. 11). Then, "you loved them" (v. 3). Now, "you sold your people for a pittance" (v. 12). For every blessing of the past the psalmist mentions a curse in the present. He has lost the rhythms of life even as the stately cadences of his poetry remain balanced and clear. His confrontation with the painful realities of today stand in sharp contrast with the comfort provided by the pleasing rhythms of the past. He is like a person trying hard to keep his equanimity while underneath seething with discontent.

Dissonance

The depth of the psalmist's anger relates to his feeling that God has let him and his people down. Note verse 17:

All this has happened to us,
  though we had not forgotten you
  or been false to your covenant.

God has deceived him. God has dropped the ball. God has become mysteriously silent. The writer feels that God is to blame for his predicament. Though God is silent, the psalmist must keep speaking. He joins a league with Jeremiah, who accused God of being a "deceitful brook" to him; with Moses, who felt God wanted to kill him; and with Job, who knew that God had rewarded him disproportionately with evil in his life. Deep down, many of us feel that we also belong in that league. We accuse God, though we are reluctant to admit it, of destroying our lives. In the language of the psalm we feel that the God of our past is somehow not big enough for the needs of the present.

Good News

The good news that comes from this psalm, and that ought to flow into our lives, is that precisely in this attitude of anger and rejection, the psalmist knows more than ever where he needs to go to complain. He is physically and spiritually exhausted and rejected, but this drives him ever more into the arms of God. He is saying, "In my distress I want you to show yourself. I want to affirm you. I am more dependent on you now in your silence than I ever was in your speaking." He is like a husband who has always sung his wife's praises and then almost loses her to illness or accident. The husband knows now more than ever before how much he needs his wife. Distress has driven the psalmist right into the arms of the God he thought had abandoned him. He believes that God is lost, figuratively speaking, but that he must rush into God's arms so that he (the psalmist) may be found. He has realized the truth that appears in another psalm, "I said to the LORD, 'You are my Lord; apart from you I have no good thing' " (Ps 16:2).

He might feel temporarily that God is the God who has brought him evil, but ultimately he recognizes that God is truly the only source of his good. He wants so badly not to be separated from God. His cry reverberates down through the ages and is graciously answered in God's gift of Christ; for the risen Christ, in giving the Great Commission to his disciples, said, "Surely I am with you always, to the very end of the age" (Mt 28:20). And the apostle Paul, after describing in glorious detail the nature of the work of Christ for us, exclaims with joy,

> For I am convinced that neither death nor life, neither angels nor demons, neither the present nor the future, nor any powers, neither height nor depth, nor anything else in all creation, will be able to separate us from the love of God that is in Christ Jesus our Lord. (Rom 8:38)

Friends, let us take heart in our apparent rejection; for by it we are stimulated to seek God anew, and in seeking God we find God, our source and stabilizer.

Prayer

O God, you are the God of my past and my present. Sadness and loss cloud my life, and I am tempted to think that you have forgotten me. Help me open my heart to you with my honest complaints. Help me call on you in my need. Help me claim your promises that you will never leave or forsake me. For I pray in the powerful name of Jesus Christ our Lord, Amen.

TEN

◇

PSALM 69:1-12

———

SINKING

For the director of music. To the tune of "Lilies." Of David.

¹*Save me, O God,*
for the waters have come up to my neck.
²*I sink in the miry depths,*
where there is no foothold.
I have come into the deep waters;
the floods engulf me.
³*I am worn out calling for help;*
my throat is parched.
My eyes fail,
looking for my God.
⁴*Those who hate me without reason*
outnumber the hairs of my head;
many are my enemies without cause,
those who seek to destroy me.

I am forced to restore
   what I did not steal.

⁵You know my folly, O God;
   my guilt is not hidden from you.

⁶May those who hope in you
   not be disgraced because of me,
O Lord, the LORD Almighty;
may those who seek you
   not be put to shame because of me,
O God of Israel.
⁷For I endure scorn for your sake,
   and shame covers my face.
⁸I am a stranger to my brothers,
   an alien to my own mother's sons;
⁹for zeal for your house consumes me,
   and the insults of those who insult you fall on me.
¹⁰When I weep and fast,
   I must endure scorn;
¹¹when I put on sackcloth,
   people make sport of me.
¹²Those who sit at the gate mock me,
   and I am the song of the drunkards.

*P*salm 69 is a psalm of immense scope and maturity, written by a person who knows that he needs God in the deepest way. A work of breathtaking honesty, it conjures up in us all the conflicting emotions of rejection and acceptance, vitriol and calm, confidence and fear, loss and gain, and guilt and forgiveness. It is quoted throughout the New Testament, especially in the accounts of the suffering of Christ. It may even have shaped Jesus' own understanding of his role as a scorned sufferer.

The first several verses of Psalm 69 describe a life that has gotten out of control. The author's fears and anxieties threaten to swallow him like the waters of the pounding surf threaten to sweep us away. We are never told how his life has become unmanageable, but he feels partially responsible for his condition. His life is unraveling before our eyes as we read the first twelve verses of the psalm. All that is left for him is a sense of desperation; his life is ebbing from him.

We are witnessing a titanic struggle between the forces of the waters, which threaten to overcome the author, and the power of God, his ultimate source of deliverance. The strength of each—the waters and God—is almost palpable as we read. Either God or the waters will win. One of the two must conquer. For a moment the author feels that the waters will win, but ultimately he will sing God's praise. We will explore that praise in the next chapter. At this juncture, I should say that the fight is no less real for having eventually been won by God; the battle is no less intense even though, by the end, the author praises God with loud songs. Join me in studying the intensity of the psalmist's struggle in Psalm 69; for it is in life's intense points that we discover the nature of our own faith and life.

Sinking

We can do no better than to start with the opening words.

Save me, O God,
   for the waters have come up to my neck.
I sink in the miry depths,
   where there is no foothold;
I have come into deep waters;
   the floods engulf me. (vv. 1-2)

The symbol of water captures the author's feeling of hopelessness. I picture him standing up to his neck in water, and I am unsure that if I avert my eyes and then turn back to him, he will still be there. His feelings of anxiety and hopelessness have reached such a fever pitch that he is uncertain whether he will survive.

As we probe the image of the waters in verses 1-2, we note two distinct feelings that the presence of water suggests. First, the psalmist feels he is *sinking* in the water. Second, he feels *engulfed* by the floods. Each image has its own power. *Sinking* emphasizes a gradual loss of control. Sinking in the *miry depths* stresses that the more we try to find a foothold, the quicker and deeper we go. On the other hand, the *floods* stress the unpredictable nature and sudden movements of the water. Floods engulf and leave in their wake only the soggy, muddy and shattered debris of what was in their path. Floods are greeted with sudden alarm; sinking is greeted with slowly growing anxiety. Floods pummel us; the miry clay sucks us in. Both leave extensive devastation and death behind them.

Sinking in the miry depths is a potent metaphor for people who feel that life has gradually gotten out of control. It captures a dominant reality for the psalmist and for us: little by little, we become *worn down* by life. Fatigue wears me down. I often feel life is a sprint and that someone keeps moving the finish line further away from me. I look at each day, and, instead of seeing its promise, I see it as the same dreary and daunting spectacle—the enervating commute, the office difficulties, and the constant concern for children's care and health. Sometimes I have no energy to make family succeed. I face the stark realities of aging parents who are turning increasingly to me for care and support when I feel that I need support more than ever before. So, I sink into the mire of despair. Like Christian in *Pilgrim's Progress*, who, heedlessly running across the field, falls into the Slough of Despond and cannot extricate himself from its sticky slime, I feel that I can never get myself out of an endless cycle of anxiety. The psalmist's opening cry is my cry: "Save me, O God, for the waters have come up to my neck. I sink in the miry depths, where there is no foothold."

Sometimes, however, it is not the slimy mire but the engulfing floods that sweep over me. The tidal waves of life hit, and I recognize immediately how few things in life are really tied down. Waves and floods overwhelm me. I face the flood of guilt. Though guilt sometimes builds in me slowly, often the full effect strikes me much like the untamed wave of the sea, and there is no escape from its fury. I also face the floods of the breakdown of health. Just before I, Bill, started writing this book, I suffered a sudden illness that made me wonder if I would die, or be reduced to a shadow of my former self, or be unable to move from the couch or rise from my bed. The floods of threatened financial ruin also are not far off. If those of us who are fully covered by health insurance worry that sudden illness or injury might impoverish us, how do those who have little or no insurance feel?

Floods and mire threaten the psalmist's life, so he calls on God. He calls and calls but gets no answer. His throat is dry, even while he is up to his neck in water. Water, water everywhere, but the psalmist is dying of thirst! Every

flickering headlight seems like a friendly rescue ship, but then it passes by in
the night. His eyes, throat and voice are worn out, and no help appears on the
horizon. To make matters worse, his enemies want to destroy him. Verse 4
reads, in part,

> Those who hate me without reason
> outnumber the hairs of my head.

Surely we know, surely even the psalmist knew, that this is an exaggeration.
No one has that many acquaintances, let alone that many enemies. But he is
describing life as it feels and not as it is analytically measured. He is saying that
the forces arrayed against him are much superior to the forces he feels he can
muster. He knows at this point that in his own strength he is not equal to the
task. Death seems inevitable.

Reasons for His Desperation

Yet his prayer continues, and even though he explores the depths of his distress
more deeply still, he keeps talking to God. In the vast sea of despair, talking
to God is his rope of hope. Hope, however, will not come in this section.
Before hope can dawn, the psalmist performs an inner self-assessment. He
brings us in to the precious thought and feeling center of his being, the inner
sanctum, the holy of holies. He shows a remarkable level of maturity and
honesty. We are on holy ground when we hear him say (verse 5):

> You know my folly, O God;
> my guilt is not hidden from you.

Usually those engaged in a battle do not admit to weakness because if they own
up to it, their opponent will exploit their weakness and emerge victorious. Even
before God we frequently parade our bravado and declare our undying loyalty
and affection for him. Yet the psalmist will have none of this attitude. He
admits his weakness and guilt to God. He knows that it would be futile for
him to try to run or hide; for God knows the secrets of his heart. He cannot
fly from God's probing searchlight. The movement in verse 5 is one of extreme
pain and recognition for the psalmist.

It is painful because he admits he is partially to blame for his condition. Even
though the enemies oppress him, and the drunkards make songs about him,
and his family rejects him; even though he had good and convincing grounds
to blame his problems on *them*, he admits his complicity and responsibility for
his distress. He knows not simply that he is a sinner, but that he has brought

his own trouble upon himself. It is painful and wrenching to realize that part of the misery of our lives is due to our carelessness, bad choices and stupidity. The psalmist is not afraid to admit this to God.

There is also a deep flash of recognition here. For the psalmist is saying, "I accept your judgment on me, a sinner, whatever it is. I have no other option but to throw myself before you and implore your mercy. Ultimately, it is only your grace, O God, that will bring me out of this." He knows deeply, as deeply as he is known by God, that God has every ground to cast him to his enemies or to ignore his plea. The psalmist knows that he has no ground to stand on to *demand* God's help. He recognizes that without God's sovereign mercy he is absolutely lost. In this brief verse he has come to grips with his deep pain and with his deeper need for God. Without the gracious intervention of God in his life now, all will be in vain. Yet, he realizes that he has no claim on that intervention. He cannot demand God's grace. He cannot demand that God loosen his bonds. He cannot demand that God make the flood waters recede or make the slimy mire turn to solid ground. All he can do is petition for help, in God's good time, on the basis of God's merciful character.

In verses 13-36 we will see how the writer, who has no claim on God's mercy, appeals to God for help. Verse 13 continues the thought of verse 5. In the meantime, however, in verses 6-12, we hear the psalmist's worry and complaint. He feels that he has acted out of zeal for God's house, yet some who hope in God might be brought to shame through his conduct. He feels alone and misunderstood. He hears the ridicule of drunkards about him. Will their songs drown out his song to God? Will their noise stifle his noise? They sing uproariously; his throat is parched. Yet he knows that he must cast his lot with God, for better or for worse.

Prayer

O God, sometimes the cares of life sneak up on me and threaten to undo me or wash me away. I sink helplessly into the waters. Reach down to me by your gracious power and draw me up from the pit, O God. Restore the joy of my salvation, and forgive all my sins. Make me glad in your service. Through Jesus Christ our Lord, Amen.

ELEVEN

◇

PSALM 69:13-36

CLIMBING OUT

¹³But I pray to you, O LORD,
   in the time of your favor;
in your great love, O God,
   answer me with your sure salvation.
¹⁴Rescue me from the mire,
   do not let me sink;
deliver me from those who hate me,
   from the deep waters.
¹⁵Do not let the floodwaters engulf me
   or the depths swallow me up
   or the pit close its mouth over me.
¹⁶Answer me, O LORD, out of the goodness of your love;
   in your great mercy turn to me.
¹⁷Do not hide your face from your servant;
   answer me quickly, for I am in trouble.
¹⁸Come near and rescue me;
   redeem me because of my foes.

¹⁹*You know how I am scorned, disgraced and shamed;*
  all my enemies are before you.
²⁰*Scorn has broken my heart*
  and has left me helpless;
I looked for sympathy, but there was none,
  for comforters, but I found none.
²¹*They put gall in my food*
  and gave me vinegar for my thirst.
²²*May the table set before them become a snare;*
  may it become retribution and a trap.
²³*May their eyes be darkened so they cannot see,*
  and their backs be bent forever.
²⁴*Pour out your wrath on them;*
  let your fierce anger overtake them.
²⁵*May their place be deserted;*
  let there be no one to dwell in their tents.
²⁶*For they persecute those you wound*
  and talk about the pain of those you hurt.
²⁷*Charge them with crime upon crime;*
  do not let them share in your salvation.
²⁸*May they be blotted out of the book of life*
  and not be listed with the righteous.

²⁹*I am in pain and distress;*
  may your salvation, O God, protect me.

³⁰*I will praise God's name in song*
  and glorify him with thanksgiving.
³¹*This will please the LORD more than an ox,*
  more than a bull with its horns and hoofs.
³²*The poor will see and be glad—*
  you who seek God, may your hearts live!
³³*The LORD hears the needy*
  and does not despise his captive people.

³⁴*Let heaven and earth praise him,*

the seas and all that move in them,
35for God will save Zion
and rebuild the cities of Judah.
Then people will settle there and possess it;
36the children of his servants will inherit it,
and those who love his name will dwell there.

*T*he image of waters captures the reality of life for the author of Psalm 69. The waters have come up to his neck; he is gradually being sucked into the slimy muck; he is about to be overwhelmed by the tidal waves. He is a man whose psychological reality is characterized by fatigue and weariness and un- believable pressure. His life is out of his control; he is at the whim of the impersonal force of the waters. These are not the life-giving waters of which the psalmist speaks elsewhere (such as the "river of delights" in Psalm 36:8); these are the swollen and muddy waters, the tumultuous and crushing waters, the slimy and slithery swamp that can kill him at any time.

The "waters," then, are the myriad forces of distress that sap his life. He is flooded with a sea of stress, with a torrent of troubles. In his distress he cries to God, but the only voice that he hears is that of the drunkards, who make him the target of their drinking songs. To make things worse, the psalmist knows that he is partially responsible for his condition. His own carelessness or zeal may actually be hurting others as well as himself. He cries desperately to God, realizing that he is fully dependent on God's mercy. Nothing he brings to God can make God act in his favor. He must stand with arms outstretched, appealing to God's grace which alone can save him.

Psalm 69:13-36 continues and concludes the psalmist's appeal to God. As we follow them, we see the psalmist's path from overwhelming despair to strong confidence in God. It is like a road map that plots the journey of the soul from the depths to the heights. Thus, the purpose of this study is to understand, in practical ways, how the psalmist moves from the depths of despair to the mountaintop of praise. In addition, we desire that you make this psalm your own by stopping whenever you want, after each paragraph or each section, and asking God to bring about in you the rhythm and balance that come from focusing on God's ability to bring us out of the depths.

There is no easy formula that can be applied in each case, but for the author of Psalm 69 the simple truth is this: when he focuses on God's mercy and God's all-powerful ability to save, he comes forth from his despair and achieves a sense of rhythm and calm and balance. When, however, he focuses on his own condition, and notices the enemies and pain all around him, he sinks deeper into pain and vindictiveness. We will see, then, that the key to restored rhythms and joyful praise is where we direct our eyes when we have troubles.

Peter experienced a similar truth in the story of Matthew 14. Jesus' disciples were crossing the Sea of Galilee in a boat. Jesus had stayed behind after feeding the five thousand so he could pray. Then he came to the disciples walking on the water. The waves were tumultuous and the going was rough for the men in the boat. They were terrified when they saw Jesus, and they exclaimed, "It's a ghost" (Mt 14:26). But Peter, ever the impetuous one, said, "Lord, if it's you, tell me to come to you on the water." Jesus told Peter to come. Peter fixed his eyes on Jesus and, amazingly, he too walked on the water. But when he took his eyes off Christ, disaster was imminent. "When he saw the wind, he was afraid and, beginning to sink, cried out, [in words reminiscent of Psalm 69:1] 'Lord, save me' " (Mt 14:30).

Peter perfectly represents the situation of the psalmist in Psalm 69. While the psalmist's eyes are directed to God, he rises from the waters and walks on them as if they were dry ground. But when he "sees the wind," by focusing on his personal pain, the oppression of his enemies and his hopeless condition, he begins to sink, like Peter, beneath the waves. He becomes frustrated and desperate again, and he wants to exact vengeance on his foes. The question that the text of Psalm 69:13-36 suggests to us today is, Where are our eyes focused? Are our eyes on God or on our circumstances?

Start with Prayer

We have a remarkable and dramatic break in the psalm at verse 13. From verses 5-12 the psalmist focused on his condition. It was a sorry situation. Now he decides that he must change his focus. Hear his simple words in verse 13,

But I pray to you, O LORD.

Though he had been praying to God all along, the focus so far had been on *his praying*—the action of recounting his distress. Now he realizes the object of that action; he is praying *to God*—the source of strength outside of himself.

Another translation of verse 13 captures this sentiment: "But as for me, my prayer is to thee, O LORD" (RSV). The psalmist realizes that he is not simply pouring out his soul on the earth or his words into the air. His prayer has wings and has flown directly to the throne of God. For the next several verses his focus is not on his condition but on God. He doesn't describe his despair, but calls on God to act. Notice the action verbs with respect to God in verses 13-18: "answer me," "rescue me," "deliver me," "do not hide your face," "come near," "redeem me." He knows that the source of his salvation is in God alone. Unless God acts, the psalmist is lost. So he directs his prayers and his attention to God.

But he realizes that if God acts for him, it will be because of God's mercy and in his good time. Note all of verse 13:

But I pray to you, O LORD,
  in the time of your favor;
in your great love, O God,
  answer me with your sure salvation.

The psalmist is a chastened man. He would like God to answer him quickly (v. 17), but knows that God's ways are not necessarily his ways nor are God's thoughts his thoughts. He appeals to God's great love (v. 13, 16) and great mercy (v. 16). It is as if the psalmist is overwhelmed now not by the waves of distress but by the waves of divine mercy. His thought life is now captivated and controlled by divine mercy. He knows God is merciful because he is heir to a tradition that teaches that God is slow to anger and abounding in faithfulness and love (Ex 34:6). When he changes the focus of his prayer to God, he is flooded with thoughts of divine ability and goodness, as if he were saying, "O God, I cry to you and when I think of you, I become lost in your goodness. You are a great God and greatly to be praised. You are good and your grace is amazing. O God, you can rescue me; it is according to your character to rescue me. I know that you will rescue me, but it will happen in your good time. To you, O God, I leave it all." That is the spirit of Psalm 69:13-18. His mountain of disaster has become a plain; his waves of tumult have become waters of divine love. He will wait for God.

Return to the Depths
But while he is waiting for deliverance, his focus returns to himself and his situation. It is only human nature for the mind to change. We are fickle creatures, and thoughts of confidence alternate with feelings of despair. Some-

times it is hard to wait very long. It is scary to notice the wind and the waves when you are waiting for God to rescue you. We see the change of his focus in verse 19:

You know how I am scorned, disgraced and shamed.

The psalmist has changed from requesting liberation to focusing on his own troubles. "You know how I am scorned," he says. When his mind returns to the pain that he is suffering, the floodgates are released. He gives himself up to his own situation and returns to the pain that grips his life. Instead of losing himself in God, he loses himself in his situation. Metaphors even fail him. He simply is helpless. He has no friends or comforters. He has no hope. He has returned to the pit out of which he started to climb. It is so easy to slip back. He took his eyes off the *active verbs* of God's care and focused on the *adjectives* and *nouns* of his condition. God's name doesn't appear. The enemies are back. They are the only ones who are active. They are in control of his life again.

Isn't this how life works? My confidence in God ebbs and flows. I cry to God, recognize his great power, exult in his mercy and leave the timing of my deliverance to God. But then, in a process that defies an easy description, I lose my focus on God and notice only *my shame* and my *enemies' action*. I become like Peter who took his eyes off the Lord and looked at the waves.

Curses on Them!

When focusing on his enemies and his hurt, the writer's powerful feelings of vengeance arise. Most commentators on this psalm denounce the psalmist for thinking unchristian thoughts at this point. But considering that his focus is back on his problems (not on God), we might expect him to cry for vengeance. The psalms are a mirror of the soul, as Martin Luther said. They show me how life really works, rather than how we *hope* it to. When my eyes are back on myself and I notice my hurts, I want to exact vengeance on those I feel are responsible for my situation. I nurse my hurts and think how much different life would be if only they had not destroyed my life. I want them to be cut off and struck blind and devastated. I want them to be pulverized. I want their names to be obliterated so that there will be no record of their existence. I want them to return to nothingness.

Returning to God

Only God can draw us out of our rhythm-breaking cycle of vengeance and despair. But I must decide to sing praise to God. If the drunkards can make up songs about me, why can't I, in my right mind, make them up about God? If the inebriate can denounce through music, why can't I praise through music? Note the resolve of the psalmist (v. 30):

    I will praise God's name in song
      and glorify him with thanksgiving.

Praise will bring him out of the vicious cycle. This will be a song of praise in ever-growing circles. First the psalmist will praise God (v. 30). Then, the "poor will see and be glad" (v. 32). Finally, all heaven and earth will praise God (v. 34). God will repair not simply the psalmist's life but the lives of the people of God (vv. 35-36). Praise will be the great integrating force of his life. It is the strong arm that will finally pull him from the clutches of the slimy muck.

When applied to the suffering and death of Christ, Psalm 69 takes on all the more poignancy and power. He was scorned; he looked for comforters and there were none; he was fed vinegar and gall upon the cross. That great day of his death, which we now call Good Friday, was when Christ was apparently swallowed up by the turbulent waters of evil. Yet, just as the psalm ends with praise, so praise was the last word in Christ's case. He rose victorious from the grave and now his message of salvation goes out in ever-growing circles to the ends of the earth. His extreme anguish was not the *ultimate* word; it was the *penultimate* word, the second-to-the-last word. So may we, who by faith fix our eyes on the risen Christ, realize that the distress we face is not God's last word to us. For we, too, will again praise God.

Prayer

O God, I turn to you because I have no good apart from you. I celebrate your mercy and your care for me. Help me call to you in my troubles; help me not let tumultuous troubles overwhelm me. Tune my heart to active waiting for you, and may a song of praise come from my lips. Through Jesus Christ our Lord, Amen.

TWELVE

◇

PSALM 88

THE ABYSS

A song. A psalm of the Sons of Korah. For the director of music. According to mahalath leannoth. *A maskil of Heman the Ezrahite.*

¹O LORD, *the God who saves me,*
  day and night I cry out before you.
²*May my prayer come before you;*
  turn your ear to my cry.

³*For my soul is full of trouble*
  and my life draws near the grave.
⁴*I am counted among those who go down to the pit;*
  I am like a man without strength.
⁵*I am set apart with the dead,*
  like the slain who lie in the grave,
  whom you remember no more,
  who are cut off from your care.

⁶*You have put me in the lowest pit,*
  in the darkest depths.
⁷*Your wrath lies heavily upon me;*
  you have overwhelmed me with all your waves.

⁸*You have taken from me my closest friends*
  and have made me repulsive to them.
I am confined and cannot escape;
  ⁹*my eyes are dim with grief.*
  I call to you, O LORD, every day;
  I spread out my hands to you.
¹⁰*Do you show your wonders to the dead?*
  Do those who are dead rise up and praise you?
¹¹*Is your love declared in the grave,*
  your faithfulness in Destruction?
¹²*Are your wonders known in the place of darkness,*
  or your righteous deeds in the land of oblivion?

¹³*But I cry to you for help, O LORD;*
  in the morning my prayer comes before you.
¹⁴*Why, O LORD, do you reject me*
  and hide your face from me?

¹⁵*From my youth I have been afflicted and close to death;*
  I have suffered your terrors and am in despair.
¹⁶*Your wrath has swept over me;*
  your terrors have destroyed me.
¹⁷*All day long they surround me like a flood;*
  they have completely engulfed me.
¹⁸*You have taken my companions and loved ones from me;*
  the darkness is my closest friend.

*T*he psalmist probes deeper depths in Psalm 88 than in any other psalm. His darkness is more impenetrable than that of Psalm 130; the weight upon him is heavier than the weight of guilt in Psalm 51; the pummeling he takes from the waters is more severe than in Psalm 69. The cumulative nature of his distress has brought him to death's door. He is not simply at the bottom of the sea; it is as if he has fallen into a thin crack in the ocean floor and gone deeper still.

In this psalm, especially in verses 3-8, we might feel as if the psalmist is already *dead* as he writes. Oh, certainly his heart still beats, and he draws the breath of life, but his *felt* reality is complete weakness: "I am like a man without strength" (v. 4). He is exhausted, immobilized, crushed, buried and forsaken. If all these things are not enough, there appears, at first glance, to be little if any hope as the psalm progresses. Unlike Psalm 102, which explores the depths of rejection in verses 3-11 then closes on a bright note; and unlike Psalms 6 and 22, which detail the psalmist's enervating suffering but end in praise to God, Psalm 88 gives us only unrelieved gloom.

There is a certain danger in studying this psalm, because the death that the psalmist feels as he writes might be contagious. If we truly enter the depths of this psalm and do not quickly try to rush back to the safe shore of praise or confidence in God, we too may become caught in the depths of the abyss. The eddying tides of the whirlpool of despair in Psalm 88 might catch us in their vortex. Yet, if we truly meet Psalm 88 in its starkness, we may learn more about the mystery of suffering and be prepared to understand more fully the suffering love of God for us. We may find, through prayerful consideration of this hopeless psalm, a glint of hope in the God who stands under us because, ultimately, he understands us.

Our focus for Psalm 88 will not be on its progression of thought (for it seems to go round and round in circles of depression) but on three themes that capture its depth: discipline, detachment and darkness. A look at each will provide structure to a most unstructured feeling and a basis for seeing a glimmer of hope at the end of Psalm 88.

Discipline

The psalmist's spiritual *discipline* is evident by his repeated cries to God. Nor-

mally, even in psalms of lament, there is only one cry to God, at the beginning
of the psalm. For example, see Psalm 61:1-2: "Hear my cry, O God; listen to
my prayer. From the ends of the earth I call to you. I call as my heart grows
faint." Or Psalm 5:1: "Give ear to my words, O LORD, consider my sighing."
The author of Psalm 88 does the same at the beginning:

O LORD, the God who saves me,
  day and night I cry out before you.
May my prayer come before you;
  turn your ear to my cry. (vv. 1-2)

In the depths of his despair he calls on the Lord. God is given many names
in Scripture—judge, rock, fortress and, even, destroyer—but the psalmist here
chooses to call him "the God who saves me." The questions in the middle part
of the psalm (vv. 10-12) show that the author is familiar with the great acts
of God's salvation toward the people. God has done wonders and righteous
deeds and has demonstrated love and faithfulness. Thus, the psalmist's appeal
to the God who saves him shows that the psalm, though written in the depths
of hopelessness, is written by one who believes that God saves. His experience
and his belief, however, are far apart.

That does not deter the psalmist from maintaining his discipline of prayer.
Note when he prays: "day and night I cry out before you." Day and night God's
hand is heavy on him. The steadiness of the burden requires a steadiness in
prayer. The psalmist is equal to this burden! He goes further than the author
of Psalm 5, "In the morning, O LORD, you hear my voice" (v. 3). He goes the
extra mile and cries to God day and night. Though one might say that his
burden is his constant preoccupation, we have good grounds for saying that
God also is his continual focus. In addition, he states three times that he prays
to God (vv. 1-2, 9, 13). He does not give up his regular discipline of approaching God, even in his extreme weakness.

So the first thing we learn about life from the deepest depths of Psalm 88
is that religious discipline suffuses the psalm. He may feel like he is tumbling
though space with nothing to stop him, but he returns to God with regularity.
Some may wryly say that it's only natural that he would come back to God
again and again, for if you are being tossed about in circles, you eventually keep
coming back to the same position and view of the world. That is, the return
to God may not mean that life is at all under control; it may simply mean that
the endless cycle of torment has brought the psalmist to the same point on the

circle. Yet we believe that his turning to God day and night, his spreading out of his hands to God, is an affirmation of life that belies the weakness he feels.

It is also instructive for us today. When I feel that I am in my depths, the best thing to maintain is a regular spiritual discipline. Keep on praying, keep on calling upon God, even though there is no immediate answer. The discipline of calling on God, morning and evening and times in between, will bear fruit. In my darkness I cannot see the mysterious plans of God. Yet God is there to hear. My part is to maintain the regularity of my approach to him. Psalm 88 helps me in this.

Detachment

The central religious dynamic of this psalm, however, is *detachment*. All the great spiritual masters from the past have maintained that the descent into the abyss entails a detachment from all things which the world holds precious. Detachment is a process in which we gradually lose or become separated from all things we have valued so that we can be fully open to work of God in our lives. Detachment is a painful process because we are so attached to the good things of this earth—to its material comforts, to our family and friends, to our own well-being. It's like pulling skin from your body or nails from your fingers or hairs from your head. The goal of detachment is to show us how much we are dependent on the world's goods for our joy and how far we must go to make God the only source of our delight.

In Psalm 88 the author gradually loses precious things. He loses his health, his sense of meaning, his friends and, he fears, his God. He begins his complaint by looking at his cumulative troubles as one big trouble.

For my soul is full of trouble. (v. 3)

He is sick in his soul. He is in deep anguish. The collective failures and losses of the past have him in a stranglehold. His soul is full of troubles, and he feels as empty as a broken vessel that has lost all its life force. The water of his life is poured out and seeps into the dusty ground, where it quickly disappears. He has no strength, and his depression is characterized by immobility.

Often when I am overwhelmed by the troubles of life, I just sit there. I am immobilized by grief and depression for two reasons. First, the pain itself is like a dead weight on me; I am pinned. Second, the conflicting demands from every side tug at me with equal force so that I cannot move of my own volition. I am like an adult who is being tugged in opposite directions by two strong, insistent children. I can't move, and I don't want to move. Demands of family, finances, work, study and leisure pull at me. The weights of grief, weariness, tension, and friction between people immobilize me. I am tugged at and weighed down at the same moment. I simply can't move, and I fall deeper into my world of distress.

The psalmist's distress also deepens. His God is distant; his friends reject him; his health is precarious; and all the terms of faith that were meaningful to him at one time now ring hollow. He cries out in anguish because these things are being taken from him. What is life if there is no health? If all our friends desert us? If we have lost our home or loved ones? If all the things we were brought up to believe now cannot be confirmed in our experience? There is only one thing to do.

Darkness

We can embrace the *darkness*. In the growing gloom of Psalm 88, the darkness becomes impenetrable. Silent night, holy night. All is calm. All is *dark*. That is the psalmist's song. The word *darkest* or *darkness* appears three times in the psalm (vv. 6, 12, 18), but the most poignant use is in verse 18:

> You have taken my companions and loved ones from me;
> the darkness is my closest friend.

No longer is his friend a person, for they all reject him. No longer can he take solace in the great acts of God's salvation or in his health, for these seem to be vain hopes. All that remains for him is darkness. The psalmist is now on the edge of life, and it is unclear whether he will leap off or be called back to the center.

One may read verse 18 in two contradictory ways. The first reading suggests that it is like a suicide note, his last words before pulling the trigger. This interpretation is based on the fact that there is a very small step between the death that the psalmist already feels and death in actuality. This interpretation suggests that by the end of the psalm hope is gone.

Yet I read Psalm 88 differently. Though the darkness is all around the psalmist, though he is on the margin of life, he is learning something of tremendous power. He is learning that, in the darkness, God is creating secret things. He is starting to learn that he is being broken or detached from all things so that God may form a new person. He sees the darkness now not as a sign that life is closing in on him, but that God is drawing him closer to himself.

In the darkness, which the psalmist sees as a friend, God will finally reveal his special glory. Thus, even in the impenetrable gloom, when all comforts and sources of earthly strength have been removed from him, the darkness beckons him on. It calls him from his immobility. He must go by faith, not by feelings, for he can see nothing. He cannot even yet say that a glimmer of light is on the horizon. The darkness is still too thick. But, strangely, the darkness is now a friend, and the pit is not so gloomy anymore. He does not and cannot yet express this in words, but the psalm closes with an inkling of the biblical notion of redemptive, meaningful suffering. It closes with a longing for truth and for God who will meet him in the darkness.

Prayer

O Lord, sometimes I descend to the pit of deepest darkness. My soul becomes full of troubles. I become immobilized by pain. I long for death itself to take me away. Be with me in the days of gloom. Help me see that the darkness around me is not dark to you. Help me cling to you with all my strength as you bring me through the depths of the abyss. Through Jesus Christ our Lord, Amen.

PART THREE

◇

LEARNING
TO TRUST
GOD

◇

THIRTEEN

◊

PSALM 90

OUR ETERNAL HOME

A prayer of Moses the man of God.

*¹Lord, you have been our dwelling place
 throughout all generations.
²Before the mountains were born
 or you brought forth the earth and the world,
 from everlasting to everlasting you are God.*

*³You turn men back to dust,
 saying, "Return to dust, O sons of men."
⁴For a thousand years in your sight
 are like a day that has just gone by,
 or like a watch in the night.*

⁵You sweep men away in the sleep of death;
  they are like the new grass of the morning—
⁶though in the morning it springs up new,
  by evening it is dry and withered.

⁷We are consumed by your anger
  and terrified by your indignation.
⁸You have set our iniquities before you,
  our secret sins in the light of your presence.
⁹All our days pass away under your wrath;
  we finish our years with a moan.
¹⁰The length of our days is seventy years—
  or eighty, if we have the strength;
yet their span is but trouble and sorrow,
  for they quickly pass, and we fly away.

¹¹Who knows the power of your anger?
  For your wrath is as great as the fear that is due you.
¹²Teach us to number our days aright,
  that we may gain a heart of wisdom.

¹³Relent, O LORD! How long will it be?
  Have compassion on your servants.
¹⁴Satisfy us in the morning with your unfailing love,
  that we may sing for joy and be glad all our days.
¹⁵Make us glad for as many days as you have afflicted us,
  for as many years as we have seen trouble.
¹⁶May your deeds be shown to your servants,
  your splendor to their children.

¹⁷May the favor of the Lord our God rest upon us;
  establish the work of our hands for us—
  yes, establish the work of our hands.

*W*hen Jesus said that unless we receive the kingdom of God like a child we cannot enter it, he was no doubt referring to a childlike attitude of trust that is essential to Christian discipleship. Young children trust. They will unwittingly expose themselves to great danger just to be with the one they love. They will believe things that are patently untrue if a parent or sibling tells it to them. As we mature, however, we lose the instinct to trust. We have been let down and hurt, even by those we love. We are deceived by people who want to exploit us for their own advantage. We learn that we have to exercise "selective trust." We wonder, as we meet people, if we can trust them. We all learn a strategy that reveals parts of ourselves to people and conceals other parts.

Our disappointment in life is not confined to people who let us down. We also often feel that God has done us wrong. Many of us bear a silent grudge against him. We blame God for the illness or death of a loved one, for an accident that befell us, for his slowness to work positive things in our life. To trust God anew means that we need to relinquish the grudge, let go of the anger and bitterness, and give up the case that many of us secretly make against God in our hearts.

But learning to trust God anew is not an automatic process. We must work through several issues before learning to trust God again with our lives. Three of our obstacles to trust, which are reflected in many of the psalms of trust we will explore together, are fear, the brevity of life and our inability to control our destiny.

I fear so many things. I am afraid that when life *is not* going well it will only get worse. I fear that when life *is* going well I am being "set up" for a disaster. I fear for my health and that of my family, for my financial well-being, for the world and the future my children will inherit.

As I get older, I also become more aware of the brevity of life. I have seen friends die in their thirties and forties. I examine my life and see all the things I want to accomplish in this life, but I don't have a clue how I'll be able to do them. It's hard for me to put myself unreservedly in God's hands when I have so much to do.

Finally, my inability to control my future is an obstacle to trusting God. Ever since I was a child I have been told that to succeed I needed go have goals and timetables. I needed to go to college and then to graduate school. I needed to put an attractive résumé together and hone my interview skills. I had to keep alert so I wouldn't "fall behind"—as if life somehow were one great race in which I was a participant. Yet I have discovered over the years that almost nothing has worked out as I was told it would. I have realized that I am almost powerless to control my future.

In the midst of these fears, I am invited to trust God. Trusting him is not easy or automatic. It takes hard thinking and discipline. This section of the book attempts to help all of us respond in joy and firm conviction to the invitation to trust that God gives us in the Scriptures. I have no doubt that the most crucial decision in our spiritual lives *after* our commitment of faith is to trust God again—to trust God *after* our first faith is shaken, *after* the woes of life have caught up to us.

Our studies of these psalms are meant to help you identify your personal obstacles to trust in God and to bring them in humility to him so that you may learn to trust him again in joy and peace. Let's turn to the first psalm of trust, Psalm 90, and learn to trust God with the pieces and the whole of our life.

Psalm 90 deals directly with two issues of trust—our mortality and our sin— and it helps us learn to trust God even amid the harsh realities of life. It is a huge psalm, not in length but in the majesty of its words. The keynote of Psalm 90 is confidence in God, but it is confidence won only after long reflection and personal struggle. The tone is sad and stately, yet the final words have a depth of hope to them. The words are written by a solemn and earnest person; yet there is a sense, in all the solemnity, that one who trusts in God can expect deep joy. Though the psalmist's words have become immortal, as he writes, he is overwhelmed by his mortality. He sings our mortality in immortal words, our impermanence in permanent words. In this psalm he has discovered the truth of himself and the truth of God, and that truth has made him free.

The psalmist learns anew three major truths: the majesty and eternity of God, the transience of human life, and the withering power of human sin. These three ideas appear repeatedly in the psalm, and we will trace them along with other significant thoughts in our study.

The Eternal Majesty
The psalm is ascribed to "Moses the man of God." While this may seem

unlikely, since most of the Psalms come from the time of David or later, there is nothing inherently improbable about it. The drama of the psalm is increased if we follow this tradition, for Moses would have composed it during Israel's wilderness wanderings. The point then would be that people who have no permanent home or dwelling place on this earth have the Lord as their true home:

Lord, you have been our dwelling place
throughout all generations. (v. 1)

Abram left Ur of the Chaldees, settled temporarily in the land of Israel and had to buy land from the indigenous people in order to have a place to bury his wife. His descendants went down to Egypt and were enslaved there. Still they longed for the land of promise and a permanent dwelling. The exodus from Egypt, the giving of the law on Sinai and the wilderness wanderings all brought them close to the promise, but Moses and those before him died without seeing that promise fulfilled. Yet Moses appropriated the fruit of the promise by faith through the simple, clear and powerful declaration in verse 1, "Lord, you have been our dwelling place throughout all generations." It is as if Moses is saying, "Yes, when we had no home in Abraham's time, you were our home. When comfortable lodging was denied our parents in Egypt, you were their home. When we lived in tents for forty years in the wilderness and moved frequently, you, O God, were our solid rock." Only those who have been on crutches truly appreciate the ability to walk; only those who have been temporarily blinded appreciate the ability to see; only those who have been displaced from home truly appreciate home.

So the psalm begins with an overwhelming confidence in God as the psalmist's and our true home. He is awestruck and grateful as he clings to the God of Israel. God has always been a home for us, the psalmist affirms, because he has always been God:

Before the mountains were born
or you brought forth the earth and the world,
from everlasting to everlasting you are God. (v. 2)

When he writes the words *you are God*, he means that God has an unlimited abundance of power and an eternity that overcomes the limitations of time. The verb tenses of the sentence are mixed, as in John 8:58 where Jesus, in a dispute with the Jews who were trying to entrap him, said, "Before Abraham was born, I am!" Not "I was" or "I existed." Nor before the mountains were brought forth you *were* God. No. You *are* God. God's eternal presence was as real for his ancestors as for the author. Therefore, God's great power, which was seen in creation, is also evident today. One of the secrets of learning to trust God is to say, "You are God," and know that the same God who brought forth the mountains and delivered the people of Israel and raised Jesus from the dead is *our* God. Today. Right now. Readily accessible to us. At the same time the phrase "you are God" captures our gratitude, awe and sense of humility. It means that we are not gods, that we have hope for today and that without God's help we can do nothing.

Reflecting on God's permanence reminds the psalmist of his own impermanence. Verses 3-6 show in graphic detail the contrast between the eternal God and transient human beings. The verses are an extended meditation on Genesis 3:19: "Dust you are and to dust you will return." This certainty of our mortality overpowers the psalmist. We have such a brief life span, and God is eternal. Fourteen lifetimes (about a thousand years) go by as quickly for God as one day goes by for us. We are like the grass that grows and withers all in one day. So awesome is the eternal majesty of God. So short is our life on the earth.

Our Sin

The contrast between God's eternity and our transience continues, but with an added element. Compounded to our mortality is our sin and God's anger at our sin. Again, the background for the thought is the story of Adam and Eve's disobedience to God in the Garden of Eden. God's anger was directed at the serpent, the man and the woman. Toil and hardship, pain and oppression is the human condition until we return to the dust from which we were originally taken (Gen 3:16-19). The authors do not mince words in either Genesis 3 or Psalm 90. The expressions in Psalm 90, however, are not gloomy pessimism but sober realism. This section of Psalm 90 penetrates to the heart of the human condition. We are mortal *and* we are sinful. We are frail *and* self-serving. We would like to be eternal and powerful, but that is what God is. And God is angry—angry because the sin of our first parents is perpetuated in our lives. We still try to hide from God's gaze. We still try to cover up the signs that death is approaching.

If we read verses 7-11 closely we are left in a dismal condition. The stately melancholy of the psalmist is overpowering. So many things limit our life. But then verse 12 strikes a different tone,

Teach us to number our days aright,
that we may gain a heart of wisdom.

This lesson we all know is true: it is the *meaning* of our days rather than the *length* of them that is valuable. We know that our days are numbered and that our sin and weakness hem us in on every side. Yet it is what we *do* with that knowledge that determines the meaning of our life.

We can, for instance, throw up our hands and say, "Since I'm going to die soon, all of life is meaningless. What I can accomplish here is so limited and minimal. Afterward I will die and be forgotten. Why even try to make things work?" Yet the attitude of the psalmist is one of trust. He is learning to trust God. He wants to learn to count his days *not* so that he can mope over how little time is left, but *so that he might gain wisdom.* The wisdom that the psalmist gains is not unlike the person who thought he or she was going to die and then miraculously came back from the precipice of death to life again. Such a person becomes grateful for every day that dawns, for every new song the birds sing. The psalmist is saying in verse 12 that if we truly grasp our mortality we can overcome that negative attitude toward life which so many of us have, and affirm without reservation that life, though short and full of pain, is a gift from God.

Thirsting Again

These deep realizations about God's eternity and our transience and sin have rekindled an incredible thirst for God in the psalmist. God, he realizes, does not reject him, even though he is sinful. God is a merciful God. God is the dwelling place. Echoing the words of another psalm, the author knows that God's anger is for a moment but his favor is for a lifetime. So he approaches God and he requests two things. First, he asks,

Satisfy us in the morning with your unfailing love. (v. 14)

He wants each day to start with fresh and convincing reminders of God's grace. Life is toilsome, painful and complex, but he knows, with God's help, he can face life with a heart full of hope and with joyful confidence.

Second, he wants God to put a sense of meaning into his work:

May the favor of the Lord our God rest upon us;
establish the work of our hands for us—
yes, establish the work of our hands. (v. 17)

Life may be short and everything around frail and perishing, but the psalmist

confidently believes that God can make his work endure. Our work may
appear routine and endless, yet God can make it firm and lasting. Here, as we
close, is the essence of biblical trust that the psalmist and we are learning. Trust
is our confidence that God will, despite our sin and weakness and inadequacies,
come to us with his grace each day and make our work endure. The psalmist
prayed that God would establish the work of his hands. We have Psalm 90
as the proof that God did so! Should we not also ask for a heart of wisdom
so that we would grasp each day aright and seek after God afresh? We will be
surprised at the grace that God wants to shed on us.

Prayer
*Lord, teach me the value of a day, the joy of your grace and the hope of having my
work established in your sight. Help me trust you in my strength and weakness. May
you be my eternal home as long as I live. Through Jesus Christ our Lord, Amen.*

FOURTEEN

◇

PSALM 139

———

SEARCHED
AND KNOWN

For the director of music. Of David. A psalm.

¹O LORD, you have searched me
 and you know me.
²You know when I sit and when I rise;
 you perceive my thoughts from afar.
³You discern my going out and my lying down;
 you are familiar with all my ways.
⁴Before a word is on my tongue
 you know it completely, O LORD.

⁵You hem me in—behind and before;
 you have laid your hand upon me.
⁶Such knowledge is too wonderful for me,

too lofty for me to attain.

⁷*Where can I go from your Spirit?*
  Where can I flee from your presence?
⁸*If I go up to the heavens, you are there;*
  if I make my bed in the depths, you are there.
⁹*If I rise on the wings of the dawn,*
  if I settle on the far side of the sea,
¹⁰*even there your hand will guide me,*
  your right hand will hold me fast.

¹¹*If I say, "Surely the darkness will hide me*
  and the light become night around me,"
¹²*even the darkness will not be dark to you;*
  the night will shine like the day,
  for darkness is as light to you.

¹³*For you created my inmost being;*
  you knit me together in my mother's womb.
¹⁴*I praise you because I am fearfully and wonderfully made;*
  your works are wonderful,
  I know that full well.
¹⁵*My frame was not hidden from you*
  when I was made in the secret place.
When I was woven together in the depths of the earth,
  ¹⁶*your eyes saw my unformed body.*
All the days ordained for me
  were written in your book
  before one of them came to be.

¹⁷*How precious to me are your thoughts, O God!*
  How vast is the sum of them!
¹⁸*Were I to count them,*
  they would outnumber the grains of sand.
When I awake,
  I am still with you.

> [19]*If only you would slay the wicked, O God!*
>   *Away from me, you bloodthirsty men!*
> [20]*They speak of you with evil intent;*
>   *your adversaries misuse your name.*
> [21]*Do I not hate those who hate you, O* LORD,
>   *and abhor those who rise up against you?*
> [22]*I have nothing but hatred for them;*
>   *I count them my enemies.*
>
> [23]*Search me, O God, and know my heart;*
>   *test me and know my anxious thoughts.*
> [24]*See if there is any offensive way in me,*
>   *and lead me in the way everlasting.*

As I studied Psalm 139 over and over, I began to see it as the answer to the desperate aimlessness and darkness of Psalm 88. Recall that Psalm 88 is the loneliest of the psalms. The author felt that he had descended into the deepest pit and the darkest depths, where he was beyond the care and hearing of God (v. 6). Forsaken by his companions, his closest friend was the darkness (v. 18). No glimmer of light appeared; the way was all obscure; the gloom and stillness of death settled over him. If anyone is touched by his abject plight or if anyone is challenged by the psalm's theological depth and psychological rawness, it is the author of Psalm 139. He might have based the very marrow of his thought upon it as he formed Psalm 139.

The overriding sentiment of Psalm 88 is that the psalmist is *lost* in impenetrable darkness, which has enveloped him and is gradually drawing the life out of him. He resides in the darkness of Sheol, where God's steadfast love is not declared (v. 11). The overriding sentiment of Psalm 139 is that the psalmist has been *found* and that in Sheol God is present and makes the darkness light: "If I make my bed in Sheol, you are there" (v. 8). God is not in the darkness in Psalm 88. In Psalm 139, however, "even the darkness will not be dark to you; the night will shine like the day, for darkness is as light to you" (v. 12). Three times in Psalm 88 *darkness* or *darkest* is used to stress the *distance* between the psalmist and God (vv. 6, 12, 18). Three times in Psalm 139:12 the words *dark* or *darkness* are used to show the certainty of God's *presence* with the psalmist and the transmutation of darkness into light.

Psalm 139 exudes overwhelming confidence and trust in God. Something dramatic has happened to the psalmist, and he now dwells comfortably and happily in the light of God. God has found him and brought him through something. The psalmist is overwhelmed with gratitude and satisfaction because God knows him and claims him. Fully known and yet fully loved, he exults in the intimacy of being known and cared for. This is a foretaste of heaven, where we will know as we have been known. Psalm 139 breathes the air of confident intimacy. The author is intoxicated by the God who is with him and will not reject him. He can't hide anything now. His longings for guidance and for vindication are likewise known to God. He will tell all. May we listen closely to him, and understand some of the passionate drive of Psalm 139.

The Joy of Being Known
In the first six verses the author stands in wonder that the God who knows his every thought, word and deed remains with him and does not reject him. The wonder of the psalmist is real, for a powerful fear of ours is that if people *really* knew who we are, they would not like us. We conceal our lust and greed and anger under the cover of polite and civil behavior. We are afraid to admit to ourselves, much less to others, who we truly are, lest we be abandoned and have to live our life alone. Yet Psalm 139 breathes a spirit that is different from that. Look at verse 1:

O LORD, *you have searched me*
    and you know me.

The psalmist probably was taught since childhood that God knew him thoroughly. He could have read in the sacred history of the people how the Lord looks not at the outward appearance but at the heart (1 Sam 16:7). Yet in Psalm 139 we receive the impression that something dramatic has occurred where the personal truth of God's intimate and loving knowledge has come home to him with fresh power. God knows him when he sits and rises, when he goes out and lies down. God knows him in the regular and irregular rhythms of his life. Verses 1-4 are reminiscent of the well-known requirement in Deuteronomy 6:6 for Israelites to impress the Word of God on their hearts. They are to talk about the divine commandments when they sit, when they walk, when they lie down and when they get up (Deut 6:7). Just as the Word of God is to be the constant preoccupation for Israel, the servant of God is the constant preoccupation of God!

At first glance, such a divine preoccupation with the psalmist may appear burdensome to him. One of Job's complaints against God was that God was *too* close to him:

Will you never look away from me,

   or let me alone even for an instant? (Job 7:19)

Job felt that God's constant, close surveillance of him was a suffocating presence, a whirlpool of torment. Job felt hemmed in, and he needed some breathing space.

Yet the psalmist, faced with the same prospect of God's closeness, exults in Psalm 139:5-6:

You hem me in—behind and before;

   you have laid your hand upon me.

Such knowledge is too wonderful for me,

   too lofty for me to attain.

Rather than feeling constrained by God's closeness, he is amazed that God desires to lavish so much attention on him. He looks at the closeness of God much like Isaiah looks at the presence of God, when the exiles return to Jerusalem. As they leave Babylon, he says,

But you will not leave in haste

   or go in flight;

for the LORD will go before you,

   the God of Israel will be your rear guard. (Is 52:12)

God "hemmed in" the returning exiles behind and before, and they were protected as they made their triumphant return to Zion. It is wonderful for the psalmist to know that he is known by the God who delivers him from the pit. He loses himself in wonder, love and praise as he contemplates God's searching presence within him.

You Are There, O God

It dawns on the psalmist that God's presence with him now is a permanent presence, and that there is no way that he can fall outside of the loving care of God. He asks two questions in verse 7:

Where can I go from your Spirit?

Where can I flee from your presence?

He asks these questions not because he wants to escape God, but because his amazement is growing at God's searching and omnipresent love. These two rhetorical questions are meant to answer the four seemingly rhetorical questions of Psalm 88:10-12. That is, in Psalm 88 the author's appeal for God to deliver him from Sheol was based on his knowledge that God's presence was *not* in Sheol. Is God's love in Sheol? was the question of Psalm 88. "No" is the expected response. In Psalm 139 the author also asks rhetorical questions. "Where can I flee from your presence?" Nowhere. Not even in Sheol? No, for "if I make my bed in the depths (Sheol), you are there." What a powerful answer to the abandonment of Psalm 88.

But there is another, even stronger point in verses 7-12. Since God is even in Sheol, and since the darkness is as light to God, the psalmist now cannot imagine how he could ever be separated from God. If God wants us badly enough to bring us out of the pit, then God will never let us go. We can hear the faint beginnings of a thought fully expressed by Paul in a great celebration of the resurrection. Paul declares,

Death has been swallowed up in victory.

Where, O death, is your victory?

Where, O death, is your sting? (1 Cor 15:54-55)

The psalmist is confident now that God will never let him go and that the final word in his life will not belong to the darkness but to the God who makes light appear amid even death.

Known Thoroughly

The psalmist cannot get away from the thought of how intimately God knows him. He looks at his body and notices its intricate shaping and its well-working parts. An intricate body argues for an intricate Creator. He feels that he bears in his body a silent testimony to the loving and intimate care that God gives to every detail on earth. Neither a sparrow falls nor a ligament is tied but God knows it thoroughly.

Once again the psalmist is overwhelmed. The thought that God knows him so well and yet does not reject him makes him lose himself in other deep truths about God:

How precious to me are your thoughts, O God!

How vast is the sum of them!
Were I to count them,
   they would outnumber the grains of the sand.
When I awake,
   I am still with you. (vv. 17-18)

Like the author of Psalm 40, who, when he began to trust, discovered the breadth of divine truth (v. 5), the author of Psalm 139, as he is comfortable with being known by God, realizes some of the vastness of God's thoughts. The image of verses 17-18 is one of him patiently and eagerly recalling and reciting great truths about God, then growing tired and falling asleep and awaking to find that his mind is still joyfully meditating on God. Sleep has been a peaceful interlude in which the thoughts of God become emblazoned yet deeper in his heart.

So he is fully known, and God still loves him. He revels in God's continual presence with him. He enjoys God's handiwork in his body. He puts himself joyfully in God's hands. He thinks of God, and his thoughts of the divine mercy multiply. He is overwhelmed by them and drifts off into sweet sleep. He wakes up to find that it is all true and that God is still with him. Confident intensity pervades these verses.

A Plea for Vindication

Most of us wish that the psalm had ended with verse 18. We don't like the spirit of hatred expressed in verses 19-22. These thoughts interrupt the confident and overflowing wonder of verses 1-18. They betray a vindictive spirit. We don't defend the psalmist for saying these things, but we surely understand him. Like the attacks on the enemies in Psalm 55 or Psalm 69, these words are a true mirror of the heart that knows that it cannot hide from God. The author is not taking judgment into his own hands; he realizes and yields to the biblical truth that vengeance belongs to God.

Perhaps, however, the psalmist has the feeling, as he closes, that his outburst of verses 19-22 was too strong. In verse 24 he says,

See if there is any offensive way in me,
   and lead me in the way everlasting.

We would like to think that in baring his soul to God in verses 19-22, he recognizes, if even in a limited way, that his hatred for some people is an "offensive way" that must be purged from him. He wants to be led in God's way. As he concludes the psalm we are left with the impression that as he learns to trust God ever more with his life, he will discover God's thought that would be expressed most powerfully by Jesus Christ in the Sermon on the Mount (Mt 5:43-44).

You have heard that it was said, "Love your neighbor and hate your enemy." But I tell you: Love your enemy and pray for those who persecute you, that you may be sons of your Father in heaven.

Prayer

O Lord, you know me. You know me thoroughly and yet you love me. I reject myself, but you do not reject me. May I rest and find confidence in the realization that I am known through and through by you. Help me to place my trust in you, for you will never let me drift away from your loving care. Through Jesus Christ our Lord, Amen.

FIFTEEN

◇

PSALM 121

———

TRUST
FOR THE
JOURNEY

A song of ascents.

[1]I lift up my eyes to the hills—
where does my help come from?
[2]My help comes from the LORD,
the Maker of heaven and earth.

[3]He will not let your foot slip—
he who watches over you will not slumber;
[4]indeed, he who watches over Israel
will neither slumber nor sleep.

[5]The LORD watches over you—
the LORD is your shade at your right hand;

⁶the sun will not harm you by day,
nor the moon by night.

⁷The Lord will keep you from all harm—
he will watch over your life;
⁸the LORD will watch over your coming and going
both now and forevermore.

*M*artin Luther, the leader of the Protestant Reformation in Germany in the sixteenth century, once said that two of his favorite non-Christian classics were the *Iliad* and the *Odyssey* by Homer. The former was powerful for Luther because it taught that life was a battle and the latter, that life was a journey.

The metaphor of life as a journey is one that has deep resonances in the Scriptures and the history of Christianity. To cite only a few examples: (1) Before the people of Israel entered into the Promised Land, they left their Egyptian slavery and wandered forty years in the wilderness. Salvation came after deliverance and journeying. (2) The chief description in the Gospels for disciples of Jesus are those who *follow* him. A disciple walks where Jesus walks and follows him in the journey, even to death. (3) The epistle to the Hebrews stresses that the Christian's life is like a specialized journey—a race. Since we are surrounded by such a great throng of cheering, supportive saints, "Let us run with perseverance the race marked out for us" (Heb 12:1). (4) One of the greatest classics of Protestant Christian devotion, *Pilgrim's Progress*, describes the Christian life as a journey from the City of Destruction to the Heavenly Jerusalem. (5) Finally, the twentieth-century poet W. H. Auden, in his Christmas oratorio *For the Time Being*, used John 14:6 and his view of the Christian life as a journey in the following memorable lines:

He is the Way. Follow him through the Land of Unlikeness;
You will see rare beasts and have unique adventures.
He is the Truth. Seek him in the Kingdom of Anxiety;
You will come to a great city that has expected your return for years.

He is the Life. Love him in the World of the Flesh;
And at your marriage all its occasions shall dance for joy.
One could cite more examples from hymns and Christian devotion which liken the Christian life to a journey. The metaphor of journey is particularly apt because it stresses movement, obstacles along the way, unexpected joys one encounters and a direction for life. When life is a journey, life has a dynamic quality to it. We meet new things; the terrain is varied; we learn to take the measure of ourselves as we face adventures and pitfalls.

Psalm 121 is a psalm of one who has just begun a journey. Like all the psalms from 120 to 134, it is called a "song of ascents." Many scholars think that these psalms were sung by Israelites as they made their religious pilgrimages to Jerusalem. As the psalmist sets out, he directs his eyes to the enduring mountains around him and wonders aloud whether he will have the necessary strength to complete the journey. As the psalm progresses, though, calm, comfortable and eloquently simple words assure us and the psalmist that the hills and the dangers that lurk there will not keep him from his desired goal. The language of Psalm 121 does not plunge to the depths of Psalm 88 or rise to the heights of Psalm 84. Rather, we have words that are firm and solid and sure, and they gradually rise in confidence, just as the journey that the psalmist takes is full of firm and sure steps as he gradually rises through the hills to the city of God.

Psalm 121 is a brief and beloved psalm that begins with anxiety and ends with brimming trust. The one taking the journey is assured that God watches over him and that not one hair from his head will fall without the permission of a loving God. Finally, it is the kind of psalm that we can easily learn and repeat as we voice our anxieties and confidence, and so learn to trust God.

An Anxious Question

The psalmist set out for the journey to Jerusalem and notices the hills:
I lift up my eyes to the hills—
  where does my help come from? (v. 1)
He raises his eyes to the hills, the symbol of all that is enduring, and wonders if there is something more enduring. He lifts his eyes from himself to the hills and raises them still higher to see if there is someone more majestic than the hills. The hills are enduring. They are also threatening and dangerous obstacles which he must overcome. Danger lies in the steep paths through the hills. Wild beasts make their homes there. Robbers lie in wait for the unsuspecting trav-

eler. As we face the journeys of our lives, we too meet hills or obstacles that deter and discourage and menace.

For example, we face the obstacle of a life out of balance. We do not set out to lose our rhythms, but we lose our calm sense of self and a center to our lives because the requirements are so demanding that we simply cannot do justice to everything. We are people of divided loyalties, which we often do not balance well. One parishioner once told me that she could not be relied on to do *anything* from September to November because of her children's soccer schedules.

We love and want to be with family. Often we have to be at work more hours than we want. Then, we have intellectual, spiritual, physical and social needs that clamor for fulfillment. We rise in the morning already exhausted because we cannot imagine how we will get through the day. We utter a brief prayer, "Lord, please help me get through this one," or "Help me over this hurdle, and I promise I will in the future try to have a more balanced life." The day's demands become huge and imposing hills in front of us.

We face the obstacle of broken relationships. As we set out on our daily journey to work and to God, we do so very consciously as injured, scarred people. We need to learn to love again, but we hesitate to extend ourselves simply because of the time it would take to love again and the hurts that will no doubt come our way if we decide to build another relationship. As we lift our eyes to the hills, we know how much energy it will take just to get through them. We wonder if we are really able to make the journey. So we cry out with the psalmist, "Where does my help come from?"

We know we need help because life lived solely by our powers is not a full life. The obstacles are daunting. In our own strength we may be able to surmount the hills, but then we may be set upon by robbers. We need another source of strength.

A Confident Response

The remainder of the psalm is a response to the question of verse one, a response that gradually grows in confidence until it reaches the supremely trusting assertion of verse 8: "the LORD will watch over your coming and going both now and forevermore." How do we get from anxiety to brimming confidence? I suggest that verses 2-8 give three clear steps in answering this question.

First, the psalmist receives encouragement from a friend. Two people speak in Psalm 121—the anxious questioner of verse 1 and the responder in verses 2-8. Some scholars have gone so far to suggest that the question of verse 1 was put to a priest or religious official before the psalmist set out, and that the priest responds in verses 2-8 with confident words. That may be, but the point to note is that words of comfort, encouragement, confidence and trust come from a friend. I cannot state too strongly how major consolation, direction, and perspective in the Christian life are often brought by friends. We are not our own. We belong to God and to others. Friends are the channel of divine blessings. Companions on the journey supply our deficiency and bring us to deeper levels of confidence in God.

Second, the friend emphasizes the constant and steady care of God. He has experienced this care:

My help comes from the LORD,
    the Maker of heaven and earth. (v. 2)

The anxious questioner wonders where he can find help in the midst of daunting fear. The friend responds, "Let me tell you what God has done for me. God is my helper, the same God who made heaven and earth." Friend gives strength to friend by drawing on the deep well of personal experience.

Then the friend states what God will do for the anxious questioner, saying perhaps, "If God is my helper, he certainly will take care of *you*." Six times in the remaining verses the friend stresses that God watches over us. God watches us, and he watches Israel. He who worked great things for the people of God is the one who will do so for us. He uses two vivid pictures in verses 3-4 to describe God's care:

He will not let your foot slip—
    he who watches over you will not slumber;
indeed, he who watches over Israel
    will neither slumber nor sleep.

God will not let us fall. That is good news. We slip on our journey when we are distracted, when we try to go too fast or when we deliberately take our eyes off the path. The author of Psalm 73 found that his foot almost slipped when he saw the arrogant prosperity of the wicked (73:2-3). We need not fear that we will lose our foothold because the Lord watches us in our journey.

The Lord is also described as the one who neither slumbers nor sleeps. He is the ruler of the day, and the sun will not smite us; he controls the night and permits no attack of the moon. In antiquity the moon was thought to have a mysterious and potent influence over the earth. The Latin word for moon, *luna*, is the root for our words *lunacy* and *lunatic* (literally one who is under control of the moon). Our God does not sleep. When Elijah confronted the prophets of Baal in the great contest on Mount Carmel to determine which god was God, Baal was silent. Elijah mocked the prophets of Baal. " 'Shout louder!' he said. 'Surely he is a god. . . . Maybe he is sleeping and must be awakened' " (1 Kings 18:27). Perhaps the psalmist was thinking of this contrast between Baal and Yahweh as he wrote.

Third, and finally, the friend mentions that God not only provides care for the beloved, but he also gives enjoyment and comfort. Certainly the theme of God the watcher is most prominent when he says:

> The LORD watches over you—
> the LORD is the shade at your right hand. (v. 5)

He encourages us to think of the benefits the shade brings. Shade brings protection, certainly, but shade brings comfort from the blazing sun and adds to the enjoyment of the day. We close with that thought (which will come to full expression in Psalm 23, where the psalmist's enjoyment of God is compared to a feast in the midst of his foes). We see that a rhythm of trust is being established in this psalm, a trust kindled by the assuring words of a friend, by the appeal to God as our watcher, and by a hint that trusting God brings not simply protection in life but enjoyment along the journey. If we say with true affection and commitment, "My help comes from the Lord, the maker of heaven and earth," we too are ready for the journey through the hills.

Prayer

O God, the hills are all around me, and they make me anxious. I need energy and protection to surmount them. Provide me, I pray, with a helpful friend, who will inspire me with words of comfort and show me the signs of your steadfast care in my daily life. May I trust you with every step I take along the path of life, as I follow in the footsteps of Jesus. Through Jesus Christ our Lord, Amen.

SIXTEEN

◇

PSALM 46

GOD
OUR REFUGE

For the director of music. Of the Sons of Korah. According to alamoth.
A song.

¹God is our refuge and strength,
  an ever-present help in trouble.
²Therefore we will not fear, though the earth give way
  and the mountains fall into the heart of the sea,
³though its waters roar and foam
  and the mountains quake with their surging.

⁴There is a river whose streams make glad the city of God,
  the holy place where the Most High dwells.
⁵God is within her, she will not fall;

God will help her at break of day.
⁶Nations are in uproar, kingdoms fall;
he lifts his voice, the earth melts.

⁷The LORD Almighty is with us;
the God of Jacob is our fortress.

⁸Come and see the works of the LORD,
the desolations he had brought on the earth.
⁹He makes wars cease to the ends of the earth;
he breaks the bow and shatters the spear,
he burns the shields with fire.
¹⁰"Be still, and know that I am God;
I will be exalted among the nations,
I will be exalted in the earth."

¹¹The LORD Almighty is with us;
the God of Jacob is our fortress.

*T*he key to spiritual balance and restored rhythms is learning to trust God in the midst of the debilitating and joyful realities of life. Trust is a confidence that God will make clear to us the meaning of our lives and that he will lead us in the good and right way. Trust may be likened to opening our arms to God and to the world, despite the fact that we have been hurt and that, in all likelihood, we will be hurt in the future. Restoring our hope and trust in God is not easy; it is usually a gradual process that must be learned. For some it may be as easy as relearning how to ride a bike after an accident or to skate after a sprained ankle. For some, however, it may be as difficult as learning to speak again after a disabling head injury. In any case, our readiness to trust God for the present and the future determines whether our spiritual rhythms will be restored.

The author of Psalm 46 has a bold and intrepid trust in God, a trust that rises above the roaring of tumultuous oceans, the crashing of mountain slides and the menacing weapons of enemies. This trust soars directly to the throne of the exalted and eternal God. Though the trust of Psalm 46 is a trust in God that rises above earthly things, it is not a psalm that is "above it all." The confident trust of the author gives him a new perspective on the life he lives, much like the author of Psalm 40 whose feet are now securely on the rock, or the author of Psalm 27 whose head is exalted above his enemies (27:6). We have the impression as the psalm closes that the psalmist is ready to re-enter, rather than escape, life, with full trust in God his refuge.

The confidence of Psalm 46 is as strong as the trust of Psalm 121, but it goes even further. Not only is God worshiped as a protector or a keeper, but he is celebrated as the God who reduces the enemies to nothing. The psalmist rests in God's strength and rejoices that God is with him. We ought to read Psalm 46 like a hymn. Its refrain is in verses 7 and 11. Some scholars feel that originally there may have been a refrain between verses 3 and 4 also, which dropped out because of the close thematic connection between them. If we look at Psalm 46 as a hymn, with verses and a refrain, it breaks down naturally into the following three parts: God over nature, God over history and silent admiration of God.

God, Supreme over Nature

The stately language and powerful imagery of verse 1 reminds us of the confident trust of Psalm 90:1. Note the similarities:

God is our refuge and strength,
an ever-present help in trouble.
Lord, you have been our dwelling place
throughout all generations.

For those who fight battles in life, God is a refuge and strength; for those without a home, God is a dwelling place. Both opening verses stress that God is sufficient to meet our present need.

The larger context of Psalm 46, then, is that of God's triumphs over threatening natural and human forces. Three ideas in verse 1 set the context for God's victory: God as our *refuge*, God as our *strength* and God as our *ever-present help*. The meaning of God as refuge finds its roots in the Old Testament idea of cities of refuge. They are described in four Old Testament passages (Num 35:6-33; Deut 4:41-43; 19:1-13; and Josh 20). Cities of refuge were six cities in the land of Israel to which a person could flee for asylum and be safe until trial in case he had killed someone unintentionally. The city of refuge was a means by which the awful cycle of violence in a society characterized by blood vengeance could be ended. The city of refuge, therefore, stood as a physical symbol of protection and safety.

When we say that God is our refuge, we confidently proclaim that we need not flee to a physical location for protection from the avenger, but that we can turn, wherever we are, to God who gives us asylum. What unexpected and welcome good news! God is readily available; he beckons us to turn to him and be saved. God's presence as a protector remains with us forever. We sing, "When other helpers fail and comforts flee, O Thou who changest not, abide with me," and we have the firm and steady assurance that God is our steady rock of refuge. So powerful is the notion of God as refuge that it is used more than a dozen times in the Psalms alone to denote the shelter we have in him.

God is our refuge and *strength*. Refuge stresses protection while strength emphasizes our fitness for battle. Our life in the world is a battle, though we fight not against flesh and blood but "against the powers of this dark world and against the spiritual forces of evil in the heavenly realms" (Eph 6:12). Martin Luther's great hymn, "A Mighty Fortress Is Our God," based upon this psalm, captures its militant, confident and humble trust and its notion of God as our strength when it says,

A mighty fortress is our God, a bulwark never failing;
Our helper he amid the flood of mortal ills prevailing.

We sing that God is sufficient for the battles we face in this life. We know, whether we admit it or not, that we need another's strength to face the battles of life. If we fight only with human weapons such as our skills and intelligence, we grow weak and feeble because our opponents are armed with spiritual weapons. But when we arm ourselves with the divine armor (Eph 6:11-17), we are ready for whatever foes cast against us. The battle is not ours but the Lord's, and the strength with which we face each day and each struggle is strength given by the powerful and gracious might of God. Without God's help we are weak and powerless, but, as Paul says, "I can do everything through him who gives me strength" (Phil 4:13). God gives his people strength. Another psalm has it that by God's help, "I can advance against a troop; with my God I can scale a wall" (Ps 18:29).

But even God's protection and strength may not avail us if God were absent at the crucial time. So the psalmist stresses that God is an *ever-present help in trouble.* A literal translation of the phrase is "a help in troubles he is found to be abundantly." God is already there working for our benefit! Though we don't see all the signs of it, or even, at times, the minutest traces of God's presence, he is always ready to help us.

Confidence in God's constant protection and strength banishes fear (v. 2). "If God is for us, who can be against us?" asks Paul (Rom 8:31). Why fear the terror of the night, troubles of the day or enemies who arise against us? Why fear deadlines or reviews or the painful scrutiny that faces us? As if to show how incompatible fear is with the life of faith, the psalmist says that even if extreme things were to happen—if the earth were to move or the waters of the sea churn uncontrollably—he would not fear. God is above the forces of nature, even when chaos threatens to engulf us.

God, Supreme over History

The thought of the swirling and foaming waters (v. 3) reminds the psalmist of a true and calm flow of water in the city of God:

There is a river whose streams make glad the city of God. (v. 4)

The city of God is Jerusalem, but Jerusalem did not have a river. But the heavenly Jerusalem of Ezekiel 47 and Revelation 22 does. The rivers of the water of life flow from the throne of God and give refreshment to all the inhabitants of the eternal city. Thus, the psalmist is merging history and eschatology, things present and things to come, to show that the protection, strength and faithfulness of God accompany us here and now as well as there and then. Rulers of the earth are like dust to God; the nations are his playthings. They vaunt themselves and rage furiously at the Lord and his people. But God merely lifts his voice and they falter. He utters a sound, and the earth melts. God brought creation into being by a word. By a word, too, all things can cease. God is highly exalted in history. The foes that beset the holy place were rebuffed and, even if once or twice they were able to take the holy city, they would be unable to take the eternal city of God where the broad river of life flows.

Silent Admiration of God

In the face of God's wondrous control over nature, history and the kings of the earth, all we can do is:

Come and see the works of the LORD. (v. 8)

It is as if we are in a plane flying low over the scene of great destruction and desolation. The war is over, brought to an end by the God who gives us strength. As we see the shattered wrecks of time, the tumultuous seas that have been stilled, the kings of the earth that have been turned back, we are exhorted,

Be still, and know that I am God;
    I will be exalted among the nations,
    I will be exalted in the earth. (v. 10)

The original meaning of this verse is for kings of the earth to stop their fighting and recognize the exalted position of God. A contemporary application is for us to stop our feverish activity and realize, once and for all, that God, the Lord in whom we trust, is utterly willing and able to subdue every foe that confronts us just as surely as he has subdued the waters and the warring kings. "Be still," he tells us. "Don't compromise your trust. Don't sink back into the sea of distress. Don't fear those who oppose you." God's power in subduing nature, history and the present foes is power that is now *ours*. So reject any alliances that weaken your trust in God, eschew any practices that compromise your confidence. Realize that you have a refuge in him, and run to him when you are pursued. Take strength from him when battle impends, knowing that his strength is yours. Be still until you realize that your true life consists in affirming and celebrating:

God is our refuge and strength,
    an ever-present help in trouble.

Prayer

Our God, you are my mighty fortress and my strong tower. I seek you as my protector and equipper for battle. When I work and fight in my own strength, I become weak and listless. Help me tap into the rich veins of your power. Raise me up to see the world from your exalted perspective, and send me back into life with verve and undiminished zeal in your service. Through Jesus Christ our Lord, Amen.

SEVENTEEN

◇

PSALM 37

DON'T WORRY—
LEARN TO TRUST!

Of David.

¹*Do not fret because of evil men*
   or be envious of those who do wrong;
²*for like the grass they will soon wither,*
   like green plants they will soon die away.

³*Trust in the LORD and do good;*
   dwell in the land and enjoy safe pasture.
⁴*Delight yourself in the LORD*
   and he will give you the desires of your heart.

⁵*Commit your way to the LORD;*
   trust in him and he will do this:

⁶He will make your righteousness shine like the dawn,
  the justice of your cause like the noonday sun.

⁷Be still before the LORD and wait patiently for him;
  do not fret when men succeed in their ways,
  when they carry out their wicked schemes.

⁸Refrain from anger and turn from wrath;
  do not fret—it leads only to evil.
⁹For evil men will be cut off,
  but those who hope in the LORD will inherit the land.

¹⁰A little while, and the wicked will be no more;
  though you look for them, they will not be found.
¹¹But the meek will inherit the land
  and enjoy great peace.

¹²The wicked plot against the righteous
  and gnash their teeth at them;
¹³but the Lord laughs at the wicked,
  for he knows their day is coming.

¹⁴The wicked draw the sword
  and bend the bow
to bring down the poor and needy,
  to slay those whose ways are upright.
¹⁵But their swords will pierce their own hearts,
  and their bows will be broken.

¹⁶Better the little that the righteous have
  than the wealth of many wicked;
¹⁷for the power of the wicked will be broken,
  but the LORD upholds the righteous.

¹⁸The days of the blameless are known to the LORD,
  and their inheritance will endure forever.

¹⁹*In times of disaster they will not wither;*
  in days of famine they will enjoy plenty.

²⁰*But the wicked will perish:*
  The LORD's *enemies will be like the beauty of the fields,*
  they will vanish—vanish like smoke.

²¹*The wicked borrow and do not repay,*
  but the righteous give generously;
²²*those the* LORD *blesses will inherit the land,*
  but those he curses will be cut off.

²³*If the* LORD *delights in a man's way,*
  he makes his steps firm;
²⁴*though he stumble, he will not fall,*
  for the LORD *upholds him with his hand.*

²⁵*I was young and now I am old,*
  yet I have never seen the righteous forsaken
  or their children begging bread.
²⁶*They are always generous and lend freely;*
  their children will be blessed.

²⁷*Turn from evil and do good;*
  then you will dwell in the land forever.
²⁸*For the* LORD *loves the just*
  and will not forsake his faithful ones.

  They will be protected forever,
  but the offspring of the wicked will be cut off;
²⁹*the righteous will inherit the land*
  and dwell in it forever.

³⁰*The mouth of the righteous man utters wisdom,*
  and his tongue speaks what is just.
³¹*The law of his God is in his heart;*

his feet do not slip.

*32The wicked lie in wait for the righteous,
    seeking their very lives;
33but the LORD will not leave them in their power
    or let them be condemned when brought to trial.*

*34Wait for the LORD
    and keep his way.
He will exalt you to inherit the land;
    when the wicked are cut off, you will see it.*

*35I have seen a wicked and ruthless man
    flourishing like a green tree in its native soil,
36but he soon passed away and was no more;
    though I looked for him, he could not be found.*

*37Consider the blameless, observe the upright;
    there is a future for the man of peace.
38But all sinners will be destroyed;
    the future of the wicked will be cut off.*

*39The salvation of the righteous comes from the LORD;
    he is their stronghold in time of trouble.
40The LORD helps them and delivers them;
    he delivers them from the wicked and saves them,
    because they take refuge in him.*

A sports reporter was interviewing Michael Jordan, superstar of the Chicago Bulls basketball team, after a hard-fought playoff victory. Jordan had not played well in the first three quarters of the game, but he exploded in the fourth quarter and led his team to victory. What was the difference, the reporter wanted to know, between Jordan's play in the first three quarters and the final quarter? Jordan thought for a moment and said that in the first three quarters he was trying too hard to do well, but "when I let the game come to me in the fourth quarter, we won."

"I let the game come to me" does not mean that Michael Jordan became uninterested or uninvolved in the game. It means, rather, that he entered the game in a new way. It points out that his ability to relax and do his best came only after a fierce personal struggle where he had tried to make things work the way he wanted but saw that such an approach was only wearing him down. "I let the game come to me," means that he was finally able to discover the rhythms of the game and let his own rhythms merge with them, and thus lead his team to victory.

The phrase "I let the game come to me" reflects not simply the athletic strategy of a great basketball player, but also a distinct approach to life. It is, at its heart, a strategy of trust. To let life come to me means that I try to discover the rhythms, pace and balance of life around me and in me, and then gently place myself into this rhythm. It is a strategy which believes that the truth of God and an abundant life arise not when I try to "make things happen" or force things into a predetermined mold but when I live in patient trust. It is not a strategy of passivity or lack of concern about the world. It recognizes that in order for lasting change to take place, in us and in others, change should be chosen rather than imposed. To let life come to me means that I live in eager and patient expectation for opportunities and challenges to arise and then gently take them up in my life.

Psalm 37 is written by a person who is learning to let life come to him. He is struggling with the mutually incompatible principles of worry and trust. As he exhorts us over and over not to fret but to trust, we recognize that the author has himself gone through great struggles with worry and trust. Every time he tells us not to worry, we know that he has told himself the same thing dozens of times. Yet the one who has fallen most frequently is often the best teacher. As we study the passionate intensity of this psalm, especially in verses 1-11, we, too, can develop a confidence and trust in God that enables life to come to us.

Before exploring the two ideas of worry and trust in Psalm 37, a few items about Psalm 37 are helpful to know. First, it is different from any of the psalms we have studied thus far. Scholars refer to it as a "wisdom psalm" since its advice and vocabulary reflect the teaching of the Wisdom literature, especially

142 / LONGING FOR GOD

Proverbs. The chief themes of this psalm, retribution for the wicked and reward for the righteous, are also the central teachings of the wisdom tradition. Wisdom, in the biblical sense, is understanding gained from years of experience observing the ways of the world. Psalm 37 is written by a man who was once young and now is old (v. 25), and it records his close observations of life.

Second, Psalm 37 also differs from the other psalms we have studied in that it is an acrostic. The stanzas of an acrostic psalm each begin with successive letters of the Hebrew alphabet. It would be like composing a twenty-six-line poem in English, each line starting with the next letter of the alphabet. One writes acrostic poems as a challenge but, more significantly, to show that the content of the poem gives comprehensive knowledge or, as we would say, knowledge from A to Z. All the passion of the psalm and its long reflection on life are carefully articulated in a given, prescribed structure.

The acrostic structure of Psalm 37 and its wisdom content invite us to see it as a comprehensive, reflective word on the essential nature of faith. It advises readers to stop worrying and begin trusting in God. Over and over again, the author traverses the same ground, and by doing so he provides us with one of the most honest and deep reflections on the tension between worrying and trust in the Scriptures.

Worry

Three times in the first eight verses the author tells us not to fret:

Do not fret because of evil men. (v. 1)

Do not fret when men succeed in their ways,

   when they carry out their wicked schemes. (v. 7)

Refrain from anger and turn from wrath;

   do not fret—it leads only to evil. (v. 8)

He exhorts us to give up our anger and not to worry because worry is destructive to us and to others. The fretting he refers to is our jealousy and envy of the prosperity, ease and injustice of other people. The anatomy of jealousy is subtle. We observe many who have become prosperous; they live luxuriously and perhaps even flaunt their wealth. They might flout the laws of the society, oppress people or act as if others don't exist. They give the impression that their wealth, power and position are as permanent as the earth.

Several conflicting thoughts arise within us. On the one hand, we wouldn't mind having the resources that they command. We envy their seeming invulnerability. We begin to yearn for the wealth they have. On the other hand, we become angry. We would like nothing better than for them be brought down a peg, as punishment for their arrogant ostentation or as retribution for their unjust treatment of people. We fret and stew and gossip and seethe, hoping against hope that they will receive their just deserts.

Our feeling toward the arrogance, prosperity and injustice of these people begins to consume us. We want to see things changed, but we feel helpless to change them. They are prospering and we are not. Their bodies are sleek and ours are weak. They seem to have life under control while we do not. Our anxiety and envy knows no bounds and has no comforter. It is here that verse 8 speaks most clearly:

Refrain from anger and turn from wrath;

do not fret—it leads only to evil.

The psalmist has been there, worrying and angry over the arrogant injustice of some people. He has learned that nursing his anger and planning revenge leads only to evil. One of the most sobering truths of life is that preoccupation with things outside of our control leads to our planning and doing of evil. Continual focus on our powerlessness leads us to thousands of attempted "minicoups" in life, when we try to wrest power from our spouse, children, coworkers or countless others who cross our path. The Scripture teaches that those who live with worry are those who contemplate evil.

Trust

But if envy and worry is so destructive to us, how do we get rid of it? How can we help not envying others or begrudging them their good fortune? Rather than taking us through a twelve-step program on learning to trust, some steps of which we have already seen in other psalms, the psalmist approaches the issue with a "Just say no" attitude. Don't worry. Trust. That is his message. At first the contrast is stark and apparently unhelpful. If worry is our problem and trust is what we need to learn, how does it help just to tell us to desist from worry and start to trust? We think that the psalmist is aware of the force of such a question and anticipates it by giving us a great variety of synonyms for trust to help us make the concept our own. Listen to the variety of exhortations in Psalm 37:

Trust in the Lord and do good. (v. 3)

Delight yourself in the LORD

and he will give you the desires of your heart. (v. 4)
Commit your way to the LORD;
    trust in him and he will do this. (v. 5)
Be still before the LORD and wait patiently for him. (v. 7)
Turn from evil and do good. (v. 27)
Wait for the LORD
    and keep his way. (v. 34)

All of these verbs (*trust, delight, commit, be still, turn, wait, keep*) carry the same
meaning in Psalm 37. Yet the variety of terms, rather than confusing us, actually helps us grasp what trust means. It shows that trust is many-faceted. It
is like the peak of a mountain that may be climbed from a number of angles.
Any one of these terms might resonate with us, while some of the others do
not have as deep a meaning. If that is the case, grasp the word that carries
meaning for you. Grasp the term and do not let it go until you are blessed!
Are you impatient? Then for the word *trust* substitute "wait for the Lord." Do
you have difficulties choosing a course of action? Then perhaps you need to
"commit your way to the Lord." Is faith a solemn and laborious duty for you?
Then you ought to "delight yourself in the Lord."

Thus the variety of words for trust is a divine gift to weak humans. Through
the variety of words we can grasp those that communicate to us about trust.
When we do that, we find that worry and envy begin to fade and trust (or *our*
word for trust) begins to play a larger and larger role in our religious vocabulary and our personal orientation. As for you, what will it be? Which word
for trust will your claim for yourself?

Prayer
*O Lord, why do I so often seek the counsel of my mind instead of the wisdom of your
Word? You tell me that worry leads to evil, and I know this is true. Banish the envy
and fretting from my life. But please do not leave me in a vacuum. Fill me with trust
and delight in you. Grant me confidence today and tomorrow that you will act in my
life in your good time. Through Jesus Christ our Lord, Amen.*

EIGHTEEN

◊

PSALM 27

———

GOD OUR LIGHT AND OUR SALVATION

Of David.

¹The LORD is my light and my salvation—
whom shall I fear?
The LORD is the stronghold of my life—
of whom shall I be afraid?
²When evil men advance against me
to devour my flesh,
when my enemies and my foes attack me,
they will stumble and fall.
³Though an army besiege me,

my heart will not fear;
though war break out against me,
    even then will I be confident.

⁴One thing I ask of the LORD,
    this is what I seek:
that I may dwell in the house of the LORD
    all the days of my life,
to gaze upon the beauty of the LORD
    and to seek him in his temple.
⁵For in the day of trouble
    he will keep me safe in his dwelling;
he will hide me in the shelter of his tabernacle
    and set me high upon a rock.
⁶Then my head will be exalted
    above the enemies who surround me;
    at his tabernacle will I sacrifice with shouts of joy;
    I will sing and make music to the LORD.

⁷Hear my voice when I call, O LORD;
    be merciful to me and answer me.
⁸My heart says of you, "Seek his face!"
    Your face, LORD, I will seek.
⁹Do not hide your face from me,
    do not turn your servant away in anger;
    you have been my helper.
Do not reject me or forsake me,
    O God my Savior.
¹⁰Though my father and mother forsake me,
    the LORD will receive me.
¹¹Teach me your way, O LORD;
    lead me in a straight path
    because of my oppressors.
¹²Do not turn me over to the desire of my foes,
    for false witnesses rise up against me,
    breathing out violence.

> [13]*I am still confident of this:*
> *I will see the goodness of the LORD*
> *in the land of the living.*
> [14]*Wait for the LORD;*
> *be strong and take heart*
> *and wait for the LORD.*

Our study of Psalm 37 showed that a variety of scriptural terms and concepts illumine the biblical notion of trust. Learning to trust God is, I am convinced, the crucial movement in the spiritual life. It brings us out of distress and into praise. But trusting God is usually a slow process, much like the process of learning. I take a few steps. Is the ground safe? Do I really want to continue the journey? Why not stay in the familiar confines of distress? Yet I know that the key to my life as a Christian is making trust a vital concept in my life. Even more than a concept, it is a practical approach to living that can affect my work and family and all of my relationships. The author of Proverbs captured the biblical understanding of trust and its potential for yielding a full life when he said:

> *Trust in the LORD with all your heart*
> *and lean not on your own understanding;*
> *in all your ways acknowledge him,*
> *and he will make your paths straight. (3:5-6)*

So, regardless of the word we choose to express our full dependence on God (*trust, commit, delight, seek,* etc.), we have the assurance that learning to trust God will yield wonderful results in our lives.

The focus in Psalm 27 is more on trust as an attitude of life than trust as a series of particular actions that we ought to perform. The attitudes that we will explore in Psalm 27 are *trust as unhurried joy* and *trust as earnest search.* These two appear contradictory but are, in fact, compatible. The former emphasizes that trust is basically an attitude of resting or of calm confidence. The latter stresses that trust is a yearning or a longing for God and for instruction in the right path. How can I calmly yearn? How can I longingly rest? I don't know. Yet both are true and essential to a balanced rhythm in my life. I need to emphasize trust as resting so as to avoid the misunderstanding that trust in God can be identified with any particular action. I need to stress trust as searching so as to remove the suspicion that trust may be synonymous with laziness or indolence. To trust God aright means that we need to practice *both* restful joy and earnest search. Let us take up Psalm 27 to see how it holds these two in tension and how its cadences resonate with our struggles to trust God fully with our lives.

Restful Joy

The opening verse of Psalm 27 resounds with the deep confidence that we saw in the first verses of Psalm 90 and Psalm 46:

The LORD is my light and my salvation—
  whom shall I fear?
The LORD is the stronghold of my life—
  of whom shall I be afraid?

The rhythm of verses 1-3 not only heightens the psalmist's joy but also shows us that it flows from a heart that has risen above many of the obstacles that keep us in distress. Notice the repetitions:

The LORD is . . . The LORD is. (v. 1)
When evil men advance . . . when my enemies . . . attack. (v. 2)
Though an army besiege . . . though war break out. (v. 3)

The repetition gives an air of solemnity and quiet confidence to the first three verses. Evil people may attack, even armies may lay siege to me, yet the Lord is my light and my salvation, the stronghold of my life, so I will not be afraid. The tone of the first three verses is similar to the brimming confidence of Psalm 11:1 and Romans 8:31.

In the LORD I take refuge.
  How then can you say to me:
  "Flee like a bird to your mountain?" (Ps 11:1)
If God is for us, who can be against us? (Rom 8:31)

That is, since the Lord is with us, our battles are the Lord's and our results are in his hands. The God who does not permit the sparrow to fall except that he knows it and who does not let one hair of our head fall without his permission, *this* God will certainly provide light for our path and strength for our battles.

This glowing confidence is the basis of the psalmist's restful joy. Described in verses 4-7, this consists of enjoying the beauty and safety of God's house and celebrating our victory over the forces of death with shouts of joy. The description of restful joy begins in verse 4:

> One thing I ask of the LORD,
>   this is what I seek:
> that I may dwell in the house of the LORD
>   all the days of my life.

A unified focus results in restful joy: "One thing I ask of the LORD." In a world where we have thousands of options and tens of thousands of choices, joy comes to those who know and who choose one thing. One of the reasons we feel frazzled by life and unable to trust is that our lives have become a haphazard collection of activities with no organizing principle or common rationale. We dash from one thing to another, and even if all of the activities are good and necessary. We still can end up feeling divided and empty. We long for the ability to restore a unified focus, have a united heart and a focused devotion. We desperately want to say at any time in any day that we are rooted deeply in a felt love of God, founded on a rhythm of trust and easy movement, anchored firmly to the one God who draws together our scattered desires into one burning and focused moment.

Jesus knew that only one thing was truly important in life:

> Seek first his [God's] kingdom and his righteousness, and all these things will be given to you as well. (Mt 6:33)

Paul perceived that only one thing was important:

> But one thing I do: Forgetting what is behind and straining toward what is ahead, I press on toward the goal to win the prize for which God has called me heavenward in Christ Jesus. (Phil 3:13-14)

Can we select the one necessary thing for us? As I look at my typical day, I have classes and meetings and phone calls and reading and some writing. Then, during the day, I switch hats and shop for food, pick up children after school, do laundry, walk the dog, feed the children, give baths, read books to children and spend time with my wife. I must do so many things that I often put good things on hold because they don't have to be done. But I pray at the beginning of the day and throughout the day, "Lord, give me a sense today that I am rooted deeply in you, that all of my activities flow from a heart that longs to be with you. Give me an expectation and sense that grace will come through the demands of life and not only when they subside."

Amid my frenetic activities, I need to learn *one thing*—that I can live joyfully in God through my activities and not in spite of them. Those whose spiritual rhythms are restored and vibrant are those who live daily from a deep center, from a sense of rootedness in God. Scripture and our experience do not deny that most of our lives we feel like torn and scattered people. Yet, even in those circumstances we can ask God to help us seek one thing: to rest joyfully in God.

Earnest Search

Sometimes the greatest truths in life are paradoxical. We have our most crea-tive thoughts when we are not trying to be creative. We do our best when we perform most effortlessly. In Jesus' words, we find our life when we give up our life.

Therefore, it should come as no surprise for us to affirm that the key to biblical trust is, at the same time, to rest joyfully and to search earnestly. We rest in God, bask in his light and luxuriate in his strength, and thus we discover the deep and unified anchor of our faith. Yet, in Psalm 27:7-14, the stress is on our trust as an earnest search.

My heart says of you, "Seek his face!"

Your face, LORD, I will seek.

Do not hide your face from me. (vv. 8-9)

Translators render verse 8 in several different ways. Another is, "To you, O my heart, he has said, seek my face" (A. A. Anderson, *Psalms*, 1:224), or "Thou hast said, 'Seek ye my face' " (RSV). One translation stresses that God exhorts the psalmist to seek, another that the psalmist exhorts himself to seek God. The uncertainty in the translation nicely captures a spiritual truth: In our search for God we are motivated by ourselves and by God, and sometimes we cannot discern the difference in the voices!

Our earnest search for God is necessary, but it runs the risk of a return to anxiety. Just as resting calmly in God might lead to indolence, so an earnest search for God might rekindle our distress. We feel that we may seek God and not find him. So, as the psalmist seeks God, possible anxieties arise:

Do not hide your face from me. . . .

Do not reject me or forsake me. (v. 9)

The distress, however, is resolved in verse 10:

Though my father and mother forsake me,

the LORD *will receive me.*

By the time the author gets to the last two verses of the psalm, his confidence returns fully. Both rest and action, quiet joy and earnest search have been affirmed. So he says,

I am still confident of this:
I will see the goodness of the LORD
in the land of the living. (v. 13)

What a wonderfully expansive note to conclude the psalm! It is tantamount to the great Puritan confidence in approaching the Scriptures, "God has yet more truth to break forth from his Word." It is the same spirit of Habakkuk the prophet when he taught that in times to come, "the earth will be filled with the knowledge of the glory of the LORD, as the waters cover the sea" (2:14). It is almost as if the psalmist, with renewed trust, is scanning the horizon for evidence that the goodness of God will break forth. Any minute now, signs of God's presence and rule on earth will appear. One need only wait (verse 14). We wait with a joyful heart, a focused mind and longing eyes. Soon the goodness of God will show itself again, and we will joyfully, longingly and restfully claim,

The LORD *is my light and my salvation—*
whom shall I fear? (v. 1)

Prayer

O Lord my God, who sent Jesus the light of the world, enlighten and protect me. Show me when and how to bask in your abundant and beautiful grace. Help me know when and how to seek your face. Give me confidence to look for your goodness as long as I live. Through Jesus Christ our Lord, Amen.

NINETEEN

◇

PSALM 91

———

THE WARRIOR
IS THE LOVER

¹*He who dwells in the shelter of the Most High*
  will rest in the shadow of the Almighty.
²*I will say of the LORD, "He is my refuge and my fortress,*
  my God, in whom I trust."

³*Surely he will save you from the fowler's snare*
  and from the deadly pestilence.
⁴*He will cover you with his feathers,*
  and under his wings you will find refuge;
  his faithfulness will be your shield and rampart.
⁵*You will not fear the terror of night,*
  nor the arrow that flies by day,
⁶*nor the pestilence that stalks in the darkness,*

nor the plague that destroys at midday..
7A thousand may fall at your side,
ten thousand at you right hand,
but it will not come near you.
8You will only observe with your eyes
and see the punishment of the wicked.

9If you make the Most High your dwelling—
even the LORD, who is my refuge—
10then no harm will befall you,
no disaster will come near your tent.
11For he will command his angels concerning you
to guard you in all your ways;
12they will lift you up in their hands,
so that you will not strike your foot against a stone.
13You will tread upon the lion and the cobra;
you will trample the great lion and the serpent.

14"Because he loves me," says the LORD, "I will rescue him;
I will protect him, for he acknowledges my name.
15He will call upon me, and I will answer him;
I will be with him in trouble,
I will deliver him and honor him.
16With long life will I satisfy him
and show him my salvation."

W henever I teach a class on the Psalms, I ask people which ones
have been most meaningful to them over the course of their lives. Normally
people say that Psalm 23 or 100 or 8 stand out to them. Occasionally, people
will mention Psalm 90 or 121 or 27. I was surprised when one man responded
without hesitation that Psalm 91 had been the most meaningful to him.

When I asked him to explain why that was the case, he told me that when
he was growing up, his father traveled a lot. Before he would go away the family

would gather in a circle, hold hands and recite this psalm. Since it described the Lord's protective care for the psalmist, it was apt for asking "traveling mercies" for his father so that he would be safe from the dangers of the highways and byways of the trip. Each time he went they claimed the promise of 91:14,

> *"Because he loves me," says the LORD, "I will rescue him.*
> *I will protect him, for he acknowledges my name."*

They closed their recitation by entrusting their father into the wise care of God. Now, fifty years later, the man could not tell the story without a catch in his throat. It was not that the psalm itself or its recitation protected his father, he knew. Rather, it was not only that God was with his father on the trips but also that, by his grace, God gave the family this psalm as a permanent gift to remember his goodness and to celebrate their closeness as a family unit.

I would like us to view Psalm 91 as God's gift to us today. It is a psalm of trust, yet it differs from many of the other psalms we have studied. While many of them stress *how* to trust or *the importance* of trusting God, Psalm 91 explores the *fruit of trust*, the results in this life for the person who trusts God. When we combine all of this with the joyful satisfaction of Psalm 23 and the heartfelt gratitude of Psalm 40, which conclude this section on trust, we will find that there is nothing left for us to do than to praise God for his goodness to us.

Still Our God

Psalm 91:1-2 contains the resonances of many other psalms. Listen first to these two verses:

> *He who dwells in the shelter of the Most High*
> *will rest in the shadow of the Almighty.*
> *I will say of the LORD, "He is my refuge and my fortress,*
> *my God, in whom I trust."*

We also hear the triumphant echoes of God as our refuge in Psalm 46:1; of God our dwelling place in Psalm 90:1; of God as our fortress in Psalm 18:2; of God our trusted Lord in Psalm 27. We are, therefore, treading familiar ground. Yet the two terms used for God in verse 1, *Most High* and *the Almighty*, draw our attention back to times far earlier than the Psalms, back to the time of Abraham. The name "Most High" for God refers to the God who gave Abram victory over Kedorlaomer in the King's Valley (Gen 14:17-20). It is a venerable title for the God who conquers foes. Thus, to dwell in the shelter of the Most High is a rich and deep way of reaffirming trust in God, who has been the people's help from time immemorial.

Likewise, "the Almighty" is the name of God first revealed to Abram in Genesis 17. In that passage God established circumcision as a covenantal institution for his people. Abram's name was changed to Abraham because he would become "the father of many nations" (Gen 17:5). When the psalmist rests in the shadow of the Almighty he is remembering the God who shows covenant faithfulness. Thus, the ancient titles for God, recalled in Psalm 91:1-2, give the psalm a powerful historic flavor. The author is sinking his roots deeply into the people's past, and he discovers that the values of the past are still potent in the present. The Almighty God of Abraham's life is also "my refuge and my fortress, my God, in whom I trust." The ancient God is still our God, is still *my* God.

Ever-Growing Celebration

Reaffirmation of personal trust in God leads to ever-growing circles of celebration. The movement of verses 3-8 is like taking off in a plane and gradually rising above the surrounding landscape. Or, to change the imagery, it is like the ever-growing circle of water that develops when a stone is thrown into the water. It is as if the psalmist, who trusts in the venerable God of the patriarchs, is now guarded by a divine protective shield as he passes through life. Danger impends, plague ravishes, and the sword threatens, but it does not come near the one who trusts God.

Two points are of special interest here. First is the little word *surely* in verse 3:

Surely he will save you from the fowler's snare.

No word *surely* appears in the Hebrew text. Instead, there is what grammarians call an emphatic pronoun before the verb. In Hebrew, the form of the verb itself tells the reader which person and gender is indicated; so a pronoun with a verb is unnecessary to clarify the meaning. When a pronoun appears, however, as here, it means "he alone" or "surely he" or "he himself." So, when the translation says, "surely he will save you," it means that God alone and no one else will save. We should note one other use of this grammatical construction. In Isaiah 53 the author is speaking of the suffering servant who will take away our sins. In Isaiah 53:4 we have, "Surely he took up our infirmities." The use of the emphatic pronoun should make us say to ourselves,

"Yes, surely he and no one else will do it. Thanks be to God."

We may say the same thing in our lives today. When we are distressed or oppressed by the myriad things that suck life out of us or destroy our rhythms, we can say "*surely* he will save." When our life is crumbling and the anxieties of the present threaten to overwhelm us, we ought to cry out, "*surely* he will save." When the voices from the past come back to accuse us of infidelity, of laziness, of worthlessness, we may say, "*surely* God will save." If God truly is "my God, in whom I trust" (91:2), then the next words from our mouth ought to be, "*surely* he will save" (91:3).

There are times, too many times, when God's promise of salvation rings hollow in our ears. I, Bill, know a family who just lost their two-year-old son in a freak tractor accident the day before Easter. While the preparations for Easter morning were under way, cries of mourning filled the hospital and the house. Parents, grandparents and friends were—and still are—inconsolable. A yawning gap, which no one has yet looked into, now exists in the lives of dozens of people. No words will bring little Will back or even heal the hearts of those who weep. But yet . . . but yet God remains God, and he is our God and the God of our children, and his salvation is still to be seen. "*Surely* he will save."

Even as we say this, we notice a second thing—the growing scope of divine protection that is in view. God will save us from "the fowler's snare" (v. 3) and the "deadly pestilence" (v. 3), and "his faithfulness will be [our] shield and rampart" (v. 4). The "fowler's snare" refers to the plots of others, hatched out to try to keep us from the course we have chosen. The "deadly pestilence" refers to accidents of nature or things that we have no control over, which can disrupt our life in an instant. From both of these God gives deliverance. Who has not experienced recovery from sickness, an accident averted at the last moment, or hundreds of little ways in which our life is protected every day? Even when a terrible accident happens, as with little Will, we have the ultimate assurance that God will not abandon us or our children.

God's protection also is there in our battles. When handmade weapons fail, God is our unique and unfailing protective shield. Psalm 91:7 is reminiscent of these triumphant words of Isaiah 40:30-31:

> Even youths grow tired and weary,
>   and young men stumble and fall;
> but those who hope in the LORD
>   will renew their strength.

They will soar on wings like eagles;
  they will run and not grow weary,
they will walk and not be faint.

Living in the Heights

The one who says "surely God" and who truly appreciates the immensity of God's protection is able to live in triumph. These verses bring out two aspects of triumphant living: an appreciation for the maternal care of God and the heroic adventure of faith.

Our protection is given over to the angels of God (vv. 11-12):

For he will command his angels concerning you
  to guard you in all your ways;
they will lift you up in their hands,
  so that you will not strike your foot against a stone.

The pleasant description of the angels who lift us up is reminiscent of other biblical pictures where the Lord is likened to a mother eagle that hovers over and under her young, spreading out her wings to catch them as they learn to fly (Ex 19:4; Deut 32:11). God's tenderness is here in full view. God will cradle us in his arms like the mother cradles a falling child. God will not simply break our fall; he catches us and keeps us unscathed.

God's maternal care strengthens us for the heroic adventure of faith:

You will tread upon the lion and the cobra;
  you will trample the great lion and the serpent. (v. 13)

We march forth in the strength of God with renewed power and urgency because we know we are in the tender arms of God. We are warriors who now face the king of beasts and the slithery serpent with supreme confidence because God is with us.

The Warrior Is the Lover

But the warrior is not a hardened, insensate killing machine, who treads over beasts and people with no conscience. The warrior we become through triumphant living is also the lover we are in the presence of God. God rescues us not because we are strong but because we are lovers:

"Because he loves me," says the LORD, *"I will rescue him." (v. 14)*

We will have more to say on love of God when we study Psalm 116. Suffice it to say now that learning to trust God brings a greater intimacy with God than we ever thought possible. In verses 14-16 three verbs stress what we do (*love*, *acknowledge* God's name, *call* upon God), while eight emphasize God's activity to us. The one who learns to trust God will find many more things that God does for us than we do for God. God wants to shower protection, presence and satisfaction on those who trust him with all their hearts.

Prayer
Our wonderful Lord, the Most High and the Almighty, the God of the human past and the God of our today, I trust in you. You have brought me faithfully on such a long journey. May I proclaim you as the only source of my goodness and recognize your hand of protection and empowerment in my life. Make me a warrior and lover for you. Through Jesus Christ our Lord, Amen.

TWENTY

◊

PSALM 23

THE SHEPHERD PSALM

A psalm of David.

¹The LORD is my shepherd, I shall not be in want.
*   ²He makes me lie down in green pastures,*
he leads me beside quiet waters,
*   ³he restores my soul.*
He guides me in paths of righteousness
*   for his name's sake.*
⁴Even though I walk
*   through the valley of the shadow of death,*
I will fear no evil,
*   for you are with me;*
your rod and your staff,
*   they comfort me.*

⁵You prepare a table before me
  in the presence of my enemies.
You anoint my head with oil;
  my cup overflows.
⁶Surely goodness and love will follow me
  all the days of my life,
and I will dwell in the house of the LORD
  forever.

I approach Psalm 23 with conflicting feelings. I feel that its meaning is so clear, so self-evident, that any attempt to clarify it is like using a flashlight to illumine the sun. I approach Psalm 23 with some fear and hesitation because I don't want my words to mar its stately beauty or detract from its enduring power. However, Psalm 23 is alluring. It is like a tall and beckoning peak for a mountain climber or a bracing, clear stream for a fisherman or a track for a distance runner. I approach it with awe and trepidation, and also with the excitement of a child opening long-expected Christmas presents. May we all open ourselves to God so that we will hear the text and so that it will kindle our hearts!

Few psalms touch us as deeply as Psalm 23. A pastor friend told of a visit he made to the hospital room of a dying man. The man lay comatose. Tubes were running in and out of his body; his vital signs were weak. The doctors let the pastor in to visit the man but cautioned him, "Don't try to communicate with him. His condition is irreversible. He's gone."

Not really knowing what to do, my friend held the man's limp hand and began to recite the Twenty-third Psalm. "The Lord is my shepherd," he intoned. Nothing. "I shall not be in want." No reaction. But as the pastor continued, he noticed that the man moved slightly. By the middle of the psalm the man's lips began to move. At the last triumphant words, "and I will dwell in the house of the LORD forever," the man was speaking the words with my friend. Soon after, he lapsed back into a coma, never to recover.

This psalm was imprinted so deeply on the man's heart that it was deeper even than the coma into which he had sunk. Spirit communed with spirit and touched chords that exist at the very foundation of our souls.

The words of Psalm 23 are also memorable because the psalm has been set to music so many times over the years. We sing, to various tunes, "The Lord's my shepherd, I'll not want, He makes me down to lie. In pastures green he leadeth me, the quiet waters by." Or, "The King of love my shepherd is, whose goodness faileth never. I nothing want if I am his and he is mine forever." Or, finally, "My shepherd will supply my need, Jehovah is his name." The tunes range from the slow and meditative to the quick and sprightly. They reinforce the power of the psalm's leading metaphors and they unite the psalm to our souls, much like a skin graft soon becomes our skin.

We will focus today on some powerful phrases that bring the psalm to life. I urge you to repeat these phrases and apply their meaning to yourself. My prayer is that you, too, will discover that this simple psalm continues to possess overwhelming power.

Sheep and Shadows
Let's start at the beginning:

The LORD is my shepherd, I shall not be in want.

One way to study this sentence is to focus on what it means when it says that God is our shepherd. We will begin, however, with what that statement implies that we are God's sheep. We are like sheep in three ways: we are prone to wander, we don't look ahead, and we often are oblivious to the dangers that threaten us.

We are prone to wander. In Handel's great oratorio, *Messiah*, the choir sings, "All we like sheep have gone astray. We have turned every man to his own way." When the choir sings, "We have turned," it takes on a carefree, giddy tone, as if in our careless turning from God we become blithely unaware of our wandering. We also don't look ahead. We live for today, whether it is as a nation that cannot address terrible budget deficits or as a people who do not realize the corrosive effects of our personal actions. We are, finally, oblivious to danger. Like the sheep, our heads are down and focused on whatever we can get into our mouths, unaware if others are plotting against us or if we are wandering close to the deadly cliff.

This is our life. This is my life. I need a shepherd who supplies all my needs, who leads me all the journey through, whose rod keeps me on the path and whose staff keeps me moving forward.

I need this kind of shepherd because I face the valley of the shadow of death.
Read verse 4:

Even though I walk
through the valley of the shadow of death,
I will fear no evil,
for you are with me;
your rod and your staff,
they comfort me.

When I was a child, I think that I feared the shadows even more than the darkness. I remember lying awake at night with the faint radiance of a street-light casting an eerie glimmer of light into my bedroom. I saw the outline of the lamp in my room. The shadow it cast on the wall was immense. As I stared at the shadow, I thought I saw it move. Imagined or not, it was scary.

Fearing the shadows is not just a childhood experience. The valley of the shadow of death comes across our lives as adults. Sometimes physical illnesses literally make us want to die. The shadow of death falls on us when we have been defeated in our battles in life and feel there is no reason to continue to live. When all that we have worked for, saved for, planned for, prepared for is taken away, whether through the whoosh of a mighty wind or the blow of injury, we go through the shadow of death. If the shadow is near, we think, death cannot be far away. Yet, the psalmist mentions that even in this situation, "You are with me." The darkness is not dark to God. It is as bright as the day. Death has been swallowed up in life through the Lord Jesus Christ. If death has lost its sting and the grave its power, what claim can the shadows have? If the reality is gone, how can the shadow continue to exist? God has overcome death and with it has dispelled the shadows of death that dance on the screens of our minds or the walls of our bedrooms.

Our spirits rise further as we recognize that God's presence is with us day and night. God leads us to sleep in green pastures, and he wakens us to walk beside quite waters. Lest we miss the rhythmic pattern of God's lordship over the days and nights of our lives, the psalmist repeats the sentiment in verse 3: "He restores my soul" (resting); "he guides me in paths of righteousness" (waking). The feeling is captured perfectly in Psalm 3:5,

I lay down and sleep;
I wake again, because the LORD sustains me.

The point is that God is the one who restores our rhythms by leading us into sleep and into waking. In "Be Thou My Vision" we sing, "Thou my best thought by day or by night, waking or sleeping thy presence, my light," affirming the same thing. Our trust in God restores our natural rhythms of sleep and work. We begin to experience and celebrate the sense of deep calm and a strong center that flows directly from the heart of Psalm 23.

God Our Host

God is not only my shepherd; he is also my host. The shepherd protects me from harm and guides me on the right path; the host welcomes me and gives me a good meal and fine accommodations.

> You prepare a table before me
>   in the presence of my enemies.
> You anoint my head with oil;
>   my cup overflows. (v. 5)

The battle rages; enemies approach. They sharpen their weapons and take aim. What does God do? He fixes a meal for us. Right in the middle of the battle, right where the action is most dangerous. The verse is so powerful because it arises as a direct response to the feeling expressed in a verse in Psalm 78.

Psalm 78, the second longest psalm, describes the history of the people of Israel until the kingship of David. When it speaks of Israel's wilderness wanderings, it stresses the disobedience of the people. They lacked food and, thinking to mock God, said, "Can God spread a table in the desert?" (v. 19). This question reverberated through the corridors of time until our author decided to give a decisive answer to it. And what an answer! God can and does spread a table for us—a sumptuous feast. The psalmist takes it even one step further. God supplies our need, not simply in the desert but also in a place of great, immediate danger. The spirit of Psalm 23:5 is like that of Paul, who says in Romans 8 that we are not simply conquerors in Christ; we are more than conquerors (Rom 8:37). We not only have a feast in the desert but we have it in the midst of enemies. And the portions are not small. We don't have to eat and run because an impending rainstorm might wash out the church picnic. Rather, "my cup overflows." Every need is taken care of amid our foes.

Thinking about foes leads to a final thought. When I think of enemies, I think of being chased. My heart pounds, sweat bathes my brow, my breath becomes a series of gasps. I've got to escape! The psalmist is also thinking about being pursued, yet he is being pursued by God. Read verse 6:

Surely goodness and love will follow me
   all the days of my life.

Oh, what a triumph! The voice at my back, the sound at my heels is the sound of the hound of heaven who pursues me all the days of my life. It is a friend who comes after me, to embrace me and wash over me with cups of goodness and buckets of love.

Don't you feel pursued at times? When I am pressured, I feel like I am being chased. My head starts to hurt. I take deep breaths. I don't know if I'll be ready on time. Even if I am ready, I worry that I will fail at the presentation. What a joy to think that the sounds I hear pursuing me are really the graciousness and love of God. They are not following to pummel me or to exhaust me, but to set a table for me, to calm me, to restore my balance and rhythms, to say, "It's OK to slow down and breathe, because I'll let you feast in the middle of life's battles."

What more can I say? God has given his invitation to the great feast while the battles of life still rage. Let's sit down to the table and sup with him. The table is every meal, but it especially points to that meal called Communion or the Lord's Supper, in which we celebrate the Christ who gave himself so that we may live.

So come to the table. The cups are brimming. The feast is prepared. Don't wait until the battle is over to sit down for the meal. The battle will never be over in this life. God calls us now. Let him be our shepherd and our host now *in the midst of life.*

Prayer

My God, I need you. I need you as my guiding shepherd; for I wander and cannot see where I'm going. I rejoice that your provisions far exceed my needs, that your grace is more than sufficient for my cares. May I take what you have prepared for me and joyfully receive the overflowing cup right now. For you are with me, now and in all the days of my life. Through Jesus Christ our Lord, Amen.

TWENTY-ONE

◇

PSALM 40

OUT
OF THE PIT

For the director of music. Of David. A psalm.

¹*I waited patiently for the* LORD;
  he turned to me and heard my cry.
²*He lifted me out of the slimy pit,*
  out of the mud and mire;
he set my feet on a rock
  and gave me a firm place to stand.
³*He put a new song in my mouth,*
  a hymn of praise to our God.
Many will see and fear
  and put their trust in the LORD.

⁴*Blessed is the man*
  who makes the LORD his trust,
who does not look to the proud,
    to those who turn aside to false gods.
⁵*Many, O LORD my God,*
    are the wonders you have done.
The things you planned for us
    no one can recount to you;
were I to speak and tell of them,
    they would be too many to declare.

⁶*Sacrifice and offering you did not desire,*
    but my ears you have pierced;
burnt offerings and sin offerings
    you did not require.
⁷*Then I said, "Here I am, I have come—*
    it is written about me in the scroll.
⁸*I desire to do your will, O my God;*
    your law is within my heart."

⁹*I proclaim righteousness in the great assembly;*
    I do not seal my lips,
    as you know, O LORD.
¹⁰*I do not hide your righteousness in my heart;*
    I speak of your faithfulness and salvation.
I do not conceal your love and your truth
    from the great assembly.

¹¹*Do not withhold your mercy from me, O LORD;*
    may your love and your truth always protect me.
¹²*For troubles without number surround me;*
    my sins have overtaken me, and I cannot see.
They are more than the hairs of my head,
    and my heart fails within me.

¹³*Be pleased, O LORD, to save me;*

O LORD, *come quickly to help me.*
14May all who seek to take my life
   be put to shame and confusion;
may all who desire my ruin
   be turned back in disgrace.
15May those who say to me, "Aha! Aha!"
   be appalled at their own shame.
16But may all who seek you
   rejoice and be glad in you;
may those who love your salvation always say,
   "*The* LORD *be exalted!*"

17Yet I am poor and needy;
   may the Lord think of me.
You are my help and my deliverer;
   O my God, do not delay.

*P*salm 40, the last psalm of trust we will study, seems an answer to the earnest cry for help of Psalm 69. The author of Psalm 40 writes as if he had the text of Psalm 69 before him or within him, and he wanted to give a dramatic and poignant reflection on the result of his patient waiting for God's salvation.

Recall the flooding waters and the sinking mire that oppressed the author of Psalm 69. Enemies surrounded him. He recognized that he was partially to blame for his plight. All he could do was to ask God, in light of his abundant love and mercy, for deliverance. Now, in Psalm 40, that deliverance has happened. God has lifted the author "out of the slimy pit, out of the mud and mire" (40:2). As his feet are planted securely on the rock, he sees the world from a new vantage point. In the words of Psalm 27, his head is exalted above the enemies who surround him (27:6). He has a new spiritual orientation and has rediscovered his rhythms. He is learning to trust God again for his life.

In Psalm 40, then, the psalmist is learning to see the world from a different perspective—from the perspective of trust in God. Our view of the world is fully dependent on where we stand. If we stand in the pit, we can only see the slimy muck around us. If we stand, however, on the high rock, we see more than the walls of our subterranean prison, and we hear more voices than our own. Psalm 40 describes the new vistas the psalmist sees once he is out of the pit of despair.

Most important, perhaps, Psalm 40 gives us a window into the mind of one who is learning to trust God. That is, Psalm 40 not only gives us the new spiritual *vista*; it gives us the *road* to the scenic overlook. In this chapter we will trace the author's thought pattern in detail. It is especially important to follow every curve of his thinking because he shows us how to move from despair to trust. I'm not suggesting that there is a simple formula here for all circumstances, but his method is useful and instructive today. Learning how to trust God is one of the most difficult, yet central, issues of the religious life. If we are aware of our inclination *not* to trust God, and prayerfully consider this great psalm, we, too, may learn how to live again in trust.

The Wait Rewarded

He had waited. The miry slime sucked at his toes (Ps 69:2). He waited for the Lord "more than watchmen wait for the morning" (Ps 130:6). He said he had waited patiently, but, like us, he was probably restless. During his wait he cried to God for deliverance. He knew that God alone, in his good time, would pull him out. In the meantime, the jeers of his oppressors must have rung in his ears. But still he would wait for God and hope in his word.

The first verses tell the results of his wait in a threefold movement: deliverance, praise and trust.

First, there is the movement of deliverance. While he was waiting—not trying to force God's hand, not trying to bargain with God in any way for his deliverance—God brought him out of his distress. He was freed at the time of God's favor (69:13), according to his great mercy (69:14). God didn't just *draw the psalmist out of* distress; God *placed him firmly* on the rock. One can be saved from drowning and then die of exposure on the beach. But God brought him out and planted him securely. The rock symbolizes the place of security and vision. Note that for the psalmist, God has done these things. He doesn't say that "God put a ladder down the well, and I clambered out" or "God helps those who help themselves." He is utterly convinced that the movement of deliverance was initiated and carried through the grace of God.

That observation leads to the second movement, praise. For the psalmist, the experience of deliverance was like hearing a new voice. The voice of God, leading to a new rhythm of trust, has drowned out the voice of fear and uncertainty which had characterized his waiting. That explains why the psalmist discovers a song.

He put a new song in my mouth,

  a hymn of praise to our God. (v. 3)

He has regained his feet and also found his voice. Instead of the litany of complaint, eloquent and touching as it is, there is now a new song of praise. He hasn't sung this song before. But God has given him the words and the voice, and he sings lustily and joyfully. The person who has been drawn out of the pit must sing a song of praise. Singing unites the heart and mind like nothing else. A song of praise is the psalmist's way of affirming that a true change has taken place, that the deliverance he has experienced has become a major part of his life.

Third, the psalmist says that others will see his deliverance and trust God. Note verse 3:

Many will see and fear

  and put their trust in the LORD.

When they hear his joyful song of praise, they will put their trust in the Lord. The result of his deliverance is their desire to trust God with their lives. How often the experiences of another guide our lives. We try to avoid their mistakes; we imitate their successes; we rejoice in their victories. This salvation has led to a song of praise, and the song of praise leads many to trust in God. We might refer to this as "unintentional evangelism"—when we proclaim with joy the things God has done for us, others want to put their trust in God. Evangelism then is not a process of trying to convince someone through eloquent arguments. It is, rather, watching God open hearts to trust him when we proclaim God's wonderful deeds in our lives. There is not one *ought* in verse 3. The psalmist's heart is unleashed in praise, and his liberated heart is an invitation to others to join in trusting God.

Now that the psalmist is learning to trust God, new worlds of spiritual truth open to him. When he stands on the high ground of trust he recognizes the breadth of God's truth in the world. Consider verse 5:

Many, O LORD my God,

  are the wonders you have done.

The things you planned for us
  no one can recount to you;
were I to speak and tell of them,
  they would be too many to declare.

All of a sudden he sees not only God's good work toward him as an individual but countless examples of God's activity in the world. Scales have dropped from his eyes. The world is alive with divine wonders. He can say, in the words of the hymn "I Sing the Mighty Power of God": "Lord, how thy wonders are displayed where'er I turn my eye." Martin Luther had a similar experience when it finally dawned on him that the righteousness of God in Romans meant God's act of reaching down and justifying the ungodly rather than God's demand that he be perfect. When Luther saw this truth (he called the righteousness of God God's active righteousness), his mind ran through Scripture to show how, for example, the love of God meant God's love for us or the grace of God meant God's grace toward us. In other words, clearing up *one* thing made *many* things clear. For the author of Psalm 40, clearing up his personal distress made the innumerable mercies of God clear to him.

Delight in God's Will

His spiritual insight is not just *broadened* by his personal experience. It is also *deepened*. Now he is able to focus on the central concept of Scripture. Read the first words of verse 6 and the words of verse 8:

Sacrifice and offering you did not desire.

I desire to do your will, O my God;
  your law is within my heart.

He sees God's handiwork everywhere. But, perhaps even more crucially, he develops an insight whose full realization will only come in the gospel. He realizes that the essence of trusting God is not offering burnt and sin offerings. Rather, the heart of true religion is to do the will of God. The law of God is no longer an external teacher; it is an internal delight. He understands instinctively and deeply what Jeremiah only hinted at:

"This is the covenant I will make with the house of Israel
  after that time," declares the LORD.

"I will put my law in their minds
  and write it on their hearts." (Jer 31:33)

Trusting God will start to revolutionize not only his religious consciousness but also the religion of Israel. One of the countless new things he could declare if he had the time (40:5) is that a new religious vision is right around the corner. That vision will include all who desire to do God's will.

See how far we have come to this point. Deliverance has led to a song of praise and to increased trust in God. Deliverance has led to a vivid appreciation of the breadth of God's goodness in the world. Finally, deliverance has brought him to the depths of religion that finds its fullest expression in Jesus Christ, who taught in John 9:4 that the essential duty of religion is to do the will of God:

As long as it is day, we must do the work of him who sent me.

Proclaiming God

There is more. Trust leads to the continual proclamation of God's story. This is implied already in the hymn of praise which the redeemed sing (v. 3), but is explained in greater detail here. Verse 10 says:

I do not hide your righteousness in my heart;

I speak of your faithfulness and salvation.

I do not conceal your love and your truth

from the great assembly.

His song of praise has led to increased trust and new spiritual insight. Now he continues to praise God by naming God's great deeds. God's work in the heart must find its way to our lips. Here the words of praise are not simply a song on his lips but a proclamation to the people of God. Praising God's name to the people of God does two things. First, it strengthens the heart of the one who proclaims. Once we start to proclaim the great works of God, we have made the step from believing in a God who saves to believing in a God who has saved *us*. If God has saved us *once*, he will do so again. Second, it strengthens the hearts of the hearers. People need reasons to keep believing since there is so much evidence in the world that Christian faith may be a fruitless exercise. People keep on believing when they hear another's story of faith. It is a prod for them and a blessing for us.

The reason that telling the story of *my* deliverance helps *their* ability to trust God is that we all have a need to trust God and people. We were created *having* to trust, and what we *had* to do then we *need* to do now. Sometimes we convince ourselves that what we really want and need is to be in control. In fact, our hearts can only be satisfied if we learn to trust unconditionally, as a baby instinctively trusts its mother. Tell *your* story of faith; *others* will thereby learn to trust God again.

The Troubles Return

Praise and proclamation, however, are not the last words of this psalm. The psalms are very realistic. They do not imagine that all problems are solved when one trusts on one occasion. Even after deliverance, praise and new spiritual insight have come, the troubles return. We are all subject to enemy attacks and sieges in the continuous battle with our sin nature. The words of Psalm 40:12, similar to those of Psalm 69:4, put it this way:

> For troubles without number surround me;
> my sins have overtaken me, and I cannot see.
> They are more than the hairs of my head,
> and my heart fails within me.

Verses 12-17 emphasize that there will be no easy answers to the problems of distress and deliverance. Those who trust God are blessed, but they are not spared from assaults. Trust is not a genie we call forth or a magic wand we wave to make life's inconveniences go away. Yet trust is the way to wholeness and to restored rhythms. Once we have been in distress, cried for help, seen our deliverance, proclaimed God's glories and developed broader and deeper spiritual understanding, we have gone through the cycle of faith. We can look back on the long journey of our life and see it as a journey toward trust in God. When distress comes again, as it does in 40:12-17, we can almost say to ourselves, "Now I need to cry to God, and then, eventually, there will come deliverance and added insight." Distress is no longer an enemy for the one who is learning to trust God. So we can understand how James boldly proclaims,

> Consider it pure joy, my brothers, whenever you face trials of many kinds, because you know that the testing of your faith develops perseverance. Perseverance must finish its work so that you may be mature and complete, not lacking anything. (Jas 1:2-4)

God wants to make us so that we lack nothing: Learning to trust God is the hardest course of study we will ever pursue. Yet it is the most rewarding. Praise God who knows our frame! Praise God who wants to teach us to trust him!

Prayer

I thank you, Lord, that you are not silent when I cry to you. You lift me out of my predicaments; you plant my feet on the solid rock; you put a new song in my mouth; you give me new insights. You are ever with me. You are the living God, and I have no good apart from you. May I daily place myself in your care and not fear when troubles come, for you are greater than they and you will deliver me. Through Jesus Christ our Lord, Amen.

PART FOUR

◇

LOVING TO PRAISE GOD

◇

TWENTY-TWO

◇

PSALM 33

———

REASONABLE PRAISE

¹*Sing joyfully to the* LORD, *you righteous;*
  it is fitting for the upright to praise him.
²*Praise the* LORD *with the harp;*
  make music to him on the ten-stringed lyre.
³*Sing to him a new song;*
  play skillfully, and shout for joy.

⁴*For the word of the* LORD *is right and true;*
  he is faithful in all he does.
⁵*The* LORD *loves righteousness and justice;*
  the earth is full of his unfailing love.

⁶*By the word of the* LORD *were the heavens made,*

their starry host by the breath of his mouth.
⁷He gathers the waters of the sea into jars;
   he puts the deep into storehouses.
⁸Let all the earth fear the LORD;
   let all the people of the world revere him.
⁹For he spoke, and it came to be;
   he commanded, and it stood firm.
¹⁰The LORD foils the plans of the nations;
   he thwarts the purposes of the peoples.
¹¹But the plans of the LORD stand firm forever,
   the purposes of his heart through all generations.

¹²Blessed is the nation whose God is the LORD,
   the people he chose for his inheritance.
¹³From heaven the LORD looks down
   and sees all mankind;
¹⁴from his dwelling place he watches
   all who live on earth—
¹⁵he who forms the hearts of all,
   who considers everything they do.
¹⁶No king is saved by the size of his army;
   no warrior escapes by his great strength.
¹⁷A horse is a vain hope for deliverance;
   despite all its great strength it cannot save.
¹⁸But the eyes of the LORD are on those who fear him,
   on those whose hope is in his unfailing love,
¹⁹to deliver them from death
   and keep them alive in famine.

²⁰We wait in hope for the LORD;
   he is our help and our shield.
²¹In him our hearts rejoice,
   for we trust in his holy name.
²²May your unfailing love rest upon us, O LORD,
   even as we put our hope in you.

*B*efore we begin the third movement, it might be helpful to think about what we mean and don't mean by *praise*. One of the greatest obstacles to full, rich and meaningful praise is the *understanding of praise* we bring to the subject. Each Christian, whether we like it or not, has absorbed a notion of praise, even before we urge ourselves to "praise the Lord." If we are uncomfortable with our inherited notion, praise of God will be a difficult practice for us.

I have often had difficulty with the idea of praising God. My image of praise, for a long time, was a senseless, anti-intellectual shouting to God that tried to drown out uncertainties in life by ever-louder affirmations of adulation. I felt that many who praised God were hypocrites: they actually disliked or distrusted God for what he had permitted to happen to them, yet they praised God, through gritted teeth, despite all. For praise to be meaningful to me, then, it had to be something that did not negate either my mind or my experience of life.

After a great deal of reflection on the Scriptures and my life, I began to see that praise of God is rooted in gratitude. An attitude of gratitude or a mood of thankfulness is at the heart of what the Scriptures mean when they urge us to praise God. The psalm we will study in the next chapter (Ps 116) asks, "How can I repay the LORD for all his goodness to me?" (v. 12).

The answer follows, "I will sacrifice a thank offering to you and call on the name of the LORD" (v. 17). Praise begins in heartfelt thanksgiving. Conversely, when Paul talks about how it was that we all turned from God, despite God's marvelous display of his power in creation, he writes, "For although they knew God, they neither glorified him as God nor *gave thanks* to him" (Rom 1:21). Ingratitude brings our ruin; gratefulness puts us in right relationship to God and all creation.

Gratitude is a choice I must make. What I mean by this is that thankfulness or gratitude is an interpretation I place on events. For most of my life, many of my experiences are not fully good or fully bad. They are mixed. The cup of my life always has liquid in it, but I choose to say whether the cup is nearly full or nearly empty. Life's experiences do not carry with them an automatic interpretive sheet or grid through which I grade them. *I decide, I choose* whether or not I will be grateful for life.

To learn to praise God means that I choose to believe that the life I live is a gift from God. Will I choose to be thankful for life? I know a little girl who is recovering from a difficult double-lung transplant. She is so grateful because she can finally breathe without a respirator. I know a father of seven children who has lost four of them to accident or disease but is thankful that God has given him three healthy children. Most of us do not face these harrowing experiences, though each of us makes choices every day whether or not we will be thankful for our lives. Will I choose to be grateful for my parents even though I know, without a doubt, that I inherited some unhealthy things from them? Will I be grateful for my spouse and family, even though I have entertained fleeting or brooding thoughts about how much better or simpler life would be without them? Will I be grateful for my position in life, even though I might be in my position because of past choices which I now regret?

Therefore, the movement of praise is fueled by gratitude: gratitude for my life, the people who surround me, the opportunities that come my way, the choices that I make today and tomorrow. Most of all, however, my gratitude arises from the Scripture's testimony that the God who created all things by his awesome power is also a God who is constantly with me. Turn with me to study Psalm 33, to rediscover roots in praise, so that we all might learn a new song of praise, a song that anchors, fuels and directs our life in Christ.

Praise for God's Awesome Power

Psalm 33 is a calm psalm of praise. The words *calm* and *praise* are not contradictory. The psalmist is calm because he has great confidence that God's awesome power and loving care are working in his favor. God is the God of creation; God is the Lord who watches our lives now. The turbulent cares which lapped against the psalmist's boat in the psalms of distress do not appear here. The desperate feelings of abandonment and the longings for revenge are also absent. For one brief, shining moment there rings out a clear note of gladness without its accompanying chord of melancholy. It is almost as if the psalmist has sung to himself, "Be still, my soul. The Lord is on thy side," and has let these words slowly seep into the marrow of his being. He is centered on God and he praises God through a calm contemplation of God's creative and governing power in the universe.

God's awesome power is captured in verse 9:

For he spoke, and it came to be;

he commanded, and it stood firm.

The psalmist is fascinated not so much by the *result* of creation as by the *process* of creation. Creation happened by the word of God. God spoke and the starry heavens appeared. God gathered the waters together. The author of Psalm 33 wants us to think back to Genesis 1 and relive the glorious expressions of God's power in that chapter. We are to learn a *new* song (33:3) by meditating on the *old* acts of God. We get the impression that the author, as he contemplates the process of creation, is truly lost in wonder, love and praise.

The great philosopher Aristotle claimed that the birth of philosophy lay in humanity's sense of wonder. G. K. Chesterton, in the twentieth century, stated that what the modern age has taken away from us is our sense of wonder. Let us therefore read and internalize the noble and stately and calm cadences of Psalm 33, for they will teach us how to recapture our sense of wonder. They will rekindle our sense of awe at the hugeness of God's creative acts. Listen to a few of the dramatic verses:

For the word of the LORD is right and true;
he is faithful in all he does. (v. 4)
He gathers the waters of the sea into jars;
he puts the deep into storehouses. (v. 7)

Unless we are able to thank God sincerely for the wonder of his created work, we will find it difficult to see his wonders in the world today. If we neglect to give thanks to God for his most visible and striking acts of power in creation, might we not also be tempted to neglect God's more "invisible" or "ambiguous" work in our lives? The beauties of creation are lavishly bestowed upon us to get us in the habit of thanking God daily for his awesome power so that, by thanking God daily for visible things, we might be led to thank him for things not yet visible.

Praise for God's Constant Presence

God's presence with us is described in verse 18:

But the eyes of the LORD are on those who fear him,
on those whose hope is in his unfailing love.

Often parents say to children, "I've got my eye on you," and the meaning is clear. Don't misbehave. Our elementary-school teachers told us that they had eyes in the back of their heads, meaning "I see what you are doing at all times. Don't try anything! You won't get away with it."

The meaning of Psalm 33:18 is different, however. Having God's eyes on us means that he shelters us from surrounding evil. The meaning is similar to Psalm 91:3:

> Surely he will save you from the fowler's snare
> and from the deadly pestilence.

The eyes of God are searching and penetrating eyes, but they are also kindly eyes. They see all there is to see about us, but they accept us nevertheless. Psalm 103:13-14 captures this sentiment perfectly,

> As a father has compassion on his children,
> so the LORD has compassion on those who fear him,
> for he knows how we are formed,
> he remembers that we are dust.

God knows our frame, yet loves us still. God knows us through and through, but he never leaves us. This knowledge was almost too good to be true for the author of Psalm 139:

> Such knowledge is too wonderful for me,
> too lofty for me to attain. (v. 6)

The God whose wondrous word is present in creation continues to guide his people in the vicissitudes of life today. What then shall we say to all this? Better yet, what shall we sing to all this? Sing a new song of praise (v. 3). It is new because it is our own song. The divine hymnal is incomplete until we add our new song of praise. Our new song will be based on old things. We will sing of God's awesome power long ago and how he made all things by his word of command. Yet, our song also will have new verses that testify to the wondrous power of God in our own day. God spoke and God still speaks. God created and God still creates. God saw and God still sees.

What better way to conclude our thoughts than with the heartfelt appeal of verses 20-22:

> We wait in hope for the LORD;
> he is our help and our shield.
> In him our hearts rejoice,
> for we trust in his holy name.
> May your unfailing love rest upon us,
> O LORD, even as we put our hope in you.

Thanks be to God!

Prayer

O Lord our God, help me choose to praise you for the wonders displayed around me. Help me praise you for my life. Even though I can interpret my past and present in so many ways, please help me to see it as a gift from you, for you are the giver of every good and perfect gift. May my praise arise from genuine gratitude in my heart, and may I sing your praise in calm and effusive words, as you give me utterance. Through Jesus Christ our Lord, Amen.

TWENTY-THREE

◇

PSALM 116

————

THE JOY OF BEING HEARD

¹*I love the* LORD, *for he heard my voice;*
  he heard my cry for mercy.
²*Because he turned his ear to me,*
  I will call on him as long as I live.

³*The cords of death entangled me,*
  the anguish of the grave came upon me;
  I was overcome by trouble and sorrow.
⁴*Then I called on the name of the* LORD:
  "O LORD, *save me!"*

⁵*The* LORD *is gracious and righteous;*
  our God is full of compassion.
⁶*The* LORD *protects the simplehearted;*
  when I was in great need, he saved me.

7Be at rest once more, O my soul.
for the LORD has been good to you.

8For you, O LORD, have delivered my soul from death,
my eyes from tears,
my feet from stumbling,
9that I may walk before the LORD
in the land of the living.
10I believed; therefore I said,
"I am greatly afflicted."
11And in my dismay I said,
"All men are liars."

12How can I repay the LORD
for all his goodness to me?
13I will lift up the cup of salvation
and call on the name of the LORD.
14I will fulfill my vows to the LORD
in the presence of all his people.

15Precious in the sight of the LORD
is the death of his saints.
16O LORD, truly I am your servant;
I am your servant, the son of your maidservant;
you have freed me from my chains.

17I will sacrifice a thank offering to you
and call on the name of the LORD.
18I will fulfill my vows to the LORD
in the presence of all his people,
19in the courts of the house of the LORD—
in your midst, O Jerusalem.

Praise the LORD.

*F*ew things can compare with the satisfaction I feel when I have been heard. To find a sympathetic ear, a knowing nod, or an affirmative embrace makes me feel that I am not alone in thinking, feeling and seeing as I do. Conversely, few things are more humiliating than being ignored, especially when I think I have something to say. The title of the reflection today relates to the joy and deep satisfaction we experience when we are convinced that God has heard us.

Confidence that God has heard us, along with gratitude, is the foundation for the movement of praise. When we know that God hears us, we know that we will never be ultimately overlooked, abandoned or rejected by God. Confidence that God has heard us gives us boldness and an expansive vision that then wants to include all of God's creation in our act of praise. Thus, as we continue to study the movement of praise in the following chapters, we will gradually expand our horizons, as with concentric circles, from praise for what God has done for us, to praise of God for his grace in creation, to exhortations to all of creation to praise God. I invite you to enter into the movement of praise, with the prayer that your vision might likewise be enlarged so that you can see God's work and praise his name, along with all of creation.

Three words capture the vibrant intimacy and confidence of Psalm 116. In the order of their appearance they are *love, hear* and *call.* "I *love* the LORD, for he *heard* my voice. . . . I will *call* upon him as long as I live" (Ps 116:1-2). Though the words appear in this order in Psalm 116, they happen, in our personal experience, in the reverse order. That is, first we call, then we are heard, and finally we love. As the Scriptures say, "We love because he first loved us" (1 Jn 4:19). When we call on God in our need, he graciously hears us and loves us without waiting for our love in return. By looking at these three aspects of our experience (calling, being heard and loving) we will bring together the three previous movements of the Psalms—longing, distress and trust— and see how they naturally lead to praise.

Call

We begin with the psalmist's description of his former situation:

> The cords of death entangled me,
>   the anguish of the grave came upon me;

I was overcome by trouble and sorrow. (v. 3)
These words penetrate deep to the center of our being. A more vivid rendering of the first phrase is "the fingers of death grabbed hold of me." *That* was the psalmist's experience. He was near to death and his energy had failed. Perhaps he even wanted to die. I cannot explain it now, but a few years ago when I suffered a sudden and virulent attack of pneumonia, I truly felt, as I was lying in the emergency room of the hospital, that I wanted to die. I am a person who loves life, who can't wait for the next day to dawn. But somehow the sinewy fingers of death had grabbed hold of me, and I wanted to live no more.

Death also stalks us in less explicit forms, through mental anguish, through the pain of being betrayed, through defeat in some of life's enervating battles. Faced with this situation, the psalmist called on God,

O LORD, *save me! (v. 4)*

What a simple, lucid, powerful and sturdy call. It doesn't brim with eloquence, but it is one of the most eloquent and direct cries to God in the Scriptures. Every word carries weight. No word is unnecessary. No more words are required.

These four words, "O LORD, save me," ought to give us great encouragement in our distress because they teach that we need neither to be eloquent nor perceptive physicians of the soul to call on God. We don't need a detailed spiritual inventory, a mile-long prayer list, a cogent analysis of our "problem." All we need is the voice to call on God for salvation. Because God is attuned to our voice, he graciously turns his ear to us. It is as if God is listening closely to us, like the doctor to the stethoscope, to hear the inner rhythms of our life. Call to God, for he will certainly hear you.

Heard

The psalmist loves God because God has *heard* his voice. The great church father Augustine, in trying to explain how God could hear Jonah in the belly of the whale, said that God heard "because the ears of God are in the heart of him who calls." God hears because God feels what we feel, only in a deeper and fuller way. When the people of Israel groaned under their oppressive slavery in Egypt, they cried out to God. "God heard their groaning and he remembered his covenant with Abraham, with Isaac and with Jacob. So God looked on the Israelites and was concerned about them" (Ex 2:24-25). This concern led God to choose Moses, reveal his name to Moses and deliver the people from the clutches of Pharaoh. Deliverance may not happen immediately, but it surely will come. For the psalmist, his deliverance is described in verse 8:

For you, O LORD, have delivered my soul from death,
   my eyes from tears,
   my feet from stumbling.

Each of these phrases progressively puts the psalmist on firmer ground. We refer to this as our trilogy of tragedy, from which God has freed us. How good it is to be freed from death! A popular liturgy from the Taizé community, sung in many Christian churches between Easter and Pentecost, begins with the soloist, "Give thanks to the LORD for he is good," and the choir responds, "Surrexit Christus . . . Alleluia" (Christ has risen . . . Alleluia). A later verse, sung by the tenor with a burst of passionate power, is "I shall not die, I shall live. Surrexit Christus . . . Alleluia." In other words, the reality of Christ's rising from the dead means that we, too, shall live with him. Death no longer has dominion over us. It tries to grab us with its strong fingers, but God is stronger still. "You, O LORD, have delivered my soul from death."

Our eyes are also delivered from tears. What a beautiful picture of the joy anticipated now but fully realized in the day of Christ, when God will "wipe every tear from their eyes" (Rev 21:4). To have our eyes delivered from tears does not mean that we will never cry again; it means that we no longer have the feeling that we weep senseless or wasted tears.

Finally, our feet have been delivered from stumbling. We have seen already, and repeat here, the great promise of Psalm 91, that if we make the Most High our dwelling, God's angels will protect us "so that you will not strike your foot against a stone" (v. 12). The path is cleared and lighted and smooth. What a joy to be heard by God!

Love

So how do we respond? In the language of Psalm 116, we love God. Other verses in Psalm 116 use different words, but they all describe the same concept. We return to our rest (v. 7) or we walk before God (v. 9) or we "lift up the cup of salvation" (v. 13) or we fulfill our vows (v. 18) or we praise the Lord (v. 19). Many words are used to describe the psalmist's love for God. *Love* is such an imprecise word in our language; it can describe anything from a personal preference (I love chocolate) to the most intimate human relationship (I love Marian; I love Judy). In an age where we value precision and clarity above all, love seems so fuzzy. Yet the psalmist can find no other word to capture his feeling now that he has called and been heard.

The Hebrew of verse 1 does not read, "I love the LORD." It simply says, "I love." Certainly "the LORD" is implied by the text, but I think it is helpful to recognize this point from language and say that the result of being heard by God is love *in general.* Certainly we love God. But why limit it to God? "I love . . . for he heard my voice." Now that God has heard me, my stance toward *life* and not simply toward God is love. The person who loves has had his or her heart engaged by God. Our soul is at rest (v. 7), and we walk before God in the land of the living (v. 9). As another biblical author says, "whether we live or die, we belong to the Lord" (Rom 14:8).

This love is even able to conquer our most fearful experience—death. The psalmist said that the "cords of death" had entangled him (v. 3). He was afraid and thought he was about to die. Yet, as he thinks about the love, graciousness and mercy of God, he says,

> Precious in the sight of the LORD
> is the death of his saints. *(v. 15)*

He has a glimpse of the great truth that "death has been swallowed up in victory" (1 Cor 15:54). Even the death he faces is not the final word, for the love of God is able to overcome that too. See what love can do!

So we love in our rest and in our work, in our vows and in our offerings of thanksgiving, in our prayer and in our praise. Love becomes the most excellent way, not simply because Paul has taught us about it (1 Cor 13), but because we feel our gratitude to God very deeply, and we desire to practice love toward God and all creation. When we love we are open to God—to be engaged by God through Scripture or others or creation. Let us love, then, for love is from God (1 Jn 4:7). Love arises from the confidence that we have been heard by God. Love gives us a fresh song of praise. Praise God who hears our voice!

Prayer

O God, I have cried to you. Sometimes it feels as if I am yelling in a soundproof room. Yet you hear me, deliver me and accompany me all the days of my life. Help me to love—to open myself to you and to the world, and to celebrate your love for me. May I lift my voice and my heart in true praise to you, the author and finisher of my faith. Through Jesus Christ our Lord, Amen.

TWENTY-FOUR

◇

PSALM 8

―――

MAJESTY

For the director of music. According to gittith. A psalm of David.

¹O LORD, our Lord,
  how majestic is your name in all the earth!

You have set your glory
  above the heavens.
²From the lips of children and infants
  you have ordained praise
because of your enemies,
  to silence the foe and the avenger.

³When I consider your heavens,
  the work of your fingers,
the moon and the stars,
  which you have set in place,
⁴what is man that you are mindful of him,

> the son of man that you care for him?
> ⁵You made him a little lower than the heavenly beings
> and crowned him with glory and honor.

> ⁶You made him ruler over the works of your hands;
>   you put everything under his feet:
> ⁷all flocks and herds,
>   and the beasts of the field,
> ⁸the birds of the air,
>   and the fish of the sea,
>   all that swim the paths of the seas.

> ⁹O LORD, our Lord,
>   how majestic is your name in all the earth!

*T*he movement of praise begins in gratitude. The spirit of gratitude is captured perfectly in a saying from the medieval German mystic Meister Eckhart: "If the only prayer you say in your whole life is 'thank you,' that would suffice." That same spirit flows forth from the story of the ten men healed of leprosy by Jesus in Luke 17:11-19. Ten lepers called on Jesus for help. Ten lepers were made clean as they headed off to the priest. Only one of them, when he saw what had happened, came back to thank Jesus. The text says, "He threw himself at Jesus' feet and thanked him" (Lk 17:16). Though we hold up the gratitude of the returning leper as an example for our lives, we do so with the awareness that nine of the people touched by God's healing hand did not return to Jesus. Gratitude is the firm foundation on which our house of faith is built; but it may be the case that nine out of ten of us who have been healed by God do not show proper gratitude. Thus, as we begin our study of Psalm 8, let us do so with the prayer that we might be like the grateful leper, who returned to Jesus with thanks after being healed by him.

Psalm 8 breathes the spirit of one who has just climbed a tall peak, and upon reaching the top, surveys the vast expanse all around, with eyes marveling at the unparalleled vista, and breaks forth into a grateful song of praise. This psalm is about the glory of God in nature, yet the author doesn't stop there. He also reflects on *who this God is,* who is so glorious in the natural sphere. He also encourages us to ask *who are the people* who claim this God for their own. So, in Psalm 8, the majesty of God does not stand alone: it invites us to look more closely at God and at ourselves. The movement of praise is rooted in gratitude, and it is gratitude to the majestic God and knowledge of ourselves that gives dynamic life to our praise.

Who Is God?

The first and last verses of Psalm 8 are identical. They bring us in and lead us out of the psalm. Verse 1 prepares our heart for the next seven verses, and verse 9 restates the interpretive key for the whole psalm.

O LORD, *our Lord,*
  how majestic is your name in all the earth! (vv. 1, 9)

God is the Lord, but God is also *our* Lord. Like Psalm 63:1, the verse that began our first study in this book ("O God, you are my God"), this psalm's first verse sounds a general call to God and then moves to specific address. The Lord is *our* Lord; the Lord is *my* Lord. God's name is not simply crowned in our hearts; it is majestic in all the earth. The small and seemingly unimportant things reveal the greatness of God. As the children's hymn "All Things Bright and Beautiful" says, "Each little flower that opens, each little bird that sings" proclaims the glorious majesty of God.

We also see God's glory in the huge things of the universe. Often when I visit the Oregon coast, I take a walk along the beach just before dark. As sunset approaches, I note the typical signs of beach activity: children running and laughing, frisbees flying, people shouting back and forth to each other. Yet as the sun dips into the ocean, all the action on the beach stops. We fall silent, almost as if we were an audience in a great symphony hall. Conversations become hushed. Children stop running. Balls are not thrown. All eyes turn to the sun until it dips below the horizon. Perfect silence reigns. The silent splendor of God's sunset has worked its magic in our hearts. After the sun slides behind the sea and everyone returns to his or her activity, I go on my way too, with this verse on my lips: "O LORD, our Lord, how majestic is your name in all the earth!"

God's glory shines above the heavens and below the heavens. The fine arrangement and beauty of moon, sun and stars show the skill of the heavenly artist. The immense grandeur of the heavens demonstrates the incomprehensible greatness of God. All the starry, spangled expanse above our heads is the work of God's "fingers" (v. 3). Thus when the fingers of death grasp at us (Ps 116:3), we can be sure that God's fingers are stronger than death's fingers.

God's fingers are also active on earth. The magicians in Pharaoh's court recognized this. Moses and Aaron, through the power of God, brought many plagues upon the Egyptians. But the Egyptian magicians did the same through their sacred arts. It was only when Moses and Aaron brought the plague of gnats, which the magicians could not imitate, that the Egyptians said, "this is the finger of God" (Ex 8:19). Heaven and earth alike are examples of God's "fingerwork."

If the heavens give inaudible testimony to God's greatness, children praise God with audible voice. Note verse 2:

> From the lips of children and infants
> you have ordained praise.

Jesus quoted this verse during his triumphal entrance into Jerusalem, when the children called out "Hosanna." When Jesus said that unless we receive the kingdom of heaven as a child, we cannot enter it, he was referring to the simple praise of God by children. God brings praise out of children's mouths—the cry of the newborn baby, the infant's inarticulate cooing, the struggling attempts of a toddler to communicate its first words to adults. All of these are praise to God, who is mighty above and beneath the heavens.

Who Are We?

As soon as we recognize the immense majesty of God, we think of our own insignificance. When we see our comparative smallness in the scheme of things, we realize that the strength of our relationship with God rests on incomprehensible grace. The psalmist says,

> When I consider your heavens,
> the work of your fingers,
> the moon and the stars,
> which you have set in place,
> what is man that you are mindful of him,
> the son of man that you care for him? (vv. 3-4)

How small are we? We all have experiences where we feel both incredibly small and very large, where we feel impotent and where we experience great power.

Yet our focus on the majesty of God threatens to extinguish us. We look up to the dizzying heights of God and wonder if we have any place in this world at all. Yet we do! We realize,

You have made him a little lower than the heavenly beings
and crowned him with glory and honor. (v. 5)

The whole tenor of the psalm thus far has stressed our smallness. Now we see, in the eyes of God, that we are huge. Our size may be halfway between an atom and a planet, but in God's sight we are almost heavenly beings. We are fearfully and wonderfully made. We possess the image and likeness of God.

Verse 5 is quoted in Hebrews 2, where it refers to Christ who was made "a little lower than the angels" but who, through his death and resurrection, was "crowned with glory and honor" (Heb 2:6-9). Thus, the fuller scriptural context of this great psalm emphasizes that God's glory is not only evident in the marvels of creation but also in the pain of redemption. God's majesty is present in the splendor of the world as well as the suffering of the Son. Creation and redemption are thus held up in the Scriptures as two places where God's handiwork is most powerfully evident.

We have also been given dominion over all the earth. Note verse 6:

You made him ruler over the works of your hands;
you put everything under his feet.

In the last several years Christians, inspired by the environmental movement, have looked anew at the charge to "rule" over all of creation. A term that has been repeatedly used, which we prefer to the term *rule,* and which captures both our control over and responsibility for creation, is *stewardship. Stewardship* is a supple biblical term that stresses the primacy of our faithfulness to God by wise management of the resources he has placed in our care.

The wonder of it all is that the God who formed the heavens and the earth, whose glory is shown in the silence of a sunset and the cry of an infant, who sustains all things by his power, actually has put his trust in us to manage the resources of the earth wisely. We are small, certainly. We are weak and confused and selfish and destructive and often hateful. Yet we are the ones on whom God is banking for the care of the wonderful creation.

But the last word belongs also to God. Lest we think that our dominion gives us the license to despoil or waste, or lest we, in our pride, think that the fate of the earth is completely in our hands, we are brought back to where we started:

O LORD, *our Lord,*
  how majestic is your name in all the earth!

Prayer

Restore my feeling of awe, O Lord, as I greet each new day. Kindle my reverence anew as the sun goes down. As I waken or work or sleep, bring the consciousness of your excellent majesty to my heart. I praise you for your greatness. May I exercise good stewardship of the gifts of your creation. Through Jesus Christ our Lord, Amen.

TWENTY-FIVE

◊

PSALM 126
———
DREAMING

A song of ascents.

¹When the LORD brought back the captives to Zion,
   we were like men who dreamed.
²*Our mouths were filled with laughter,*
   our tongues with songs of joy.
   Then it was said among the nations,
   "The LORD has done great things for them."
³*The LORD has done great things for us,*
   and we are filled with joy.

⁴*Restore our fortunes, O LORD,*
   like streams in the Negev.
⁵*Those who sow in tears*

will reap with songs of joy.
⁶He who goes out weeping,
carrying seed to sow,
will return with songs of joy,
carrying sheaves with him.

P   *salm 126 celebrates the joy of unexpected good fortune. It throbs with the* emotion of an unexpected and sudden reversal of expectations which has happened to the people of God.

The Throb of Wondering Gratitude

To understand this reversal, we must understand a pivotal experience for the people of Israel—the exile of the leaders of Judah to Babylon in 587 B.C. Through Nebuchadnezzar's fierce assault on Jerusalem, the Jewish temple was destroyed, sacrifice was discontinued and the leaders of the people were removed to Babylon to prevent the possibility of Jewish revolt. The remaining Jews were left in dire straits. Both exiles and residents of Jerusalem were desperate. In one of the most moving psalms of exile (Psalm 137), the author plaintively describes the abuse and ridicule the exiled Jews faced in Babylon. Their captors commanded sardonically, "Sing us one of the songs of Zion," to which the Jews lamented, "How can we sing the songs of the LORD while in a foreign land?" (Ps 137:1-4).

Exile was such a humiliation, such an apparent contradiction to everything God had promised the people. Hundreds of years previously, God had promised Abraham that his descendants would occupy the land of Palestine. Isaiah the prophet had proudly proclaimed the enduring power of God in Jerusalem. The promises to David talked about an eternal kingdom under the authority of his children. Everything politically, socially and theologically seemed to point to continued Hebrew existence *and* independence in Palestine.

Some of Israel, the northern parts, had fallen to the menace of Assyria in 721 B.C. But to a people who had always held Jerusalem sacred, its destruction was sad but not ultimately corrosive to faith. Yet when the temple fell, when

the city of God crumbled and when the elite of Israelite leaders crossed the
Jordan River heading east apparently for the last time, then the floodgates of
tears opened. "Look around and see. Is any suffering like my suffering that was
inflicted on me, that the LORD brought on me in the day of his fierce anger?"
(Lam 1:12).

Exile was not only a huge humiliation; it also appeared final. Like the slam
of a door at the end of an Ibsen play or the rolling of the stone against the
opening of Jesus' tomb, the exile seemed so irreversible. For who could stand
up to the power of Nebuchadnezzar, that sovereign who was immortalized by
further conquests as well as by his hanging gardens, one of the seven wonders
of the ancient world? Who could stand against proud Babylon, which boasted
rulers dating back to Hammurabi, rulers who had taught the entire ancient
Near East the nature and function of law in a society? Who could resist the
armies of Babylon, which as recently as 612 B.C. had sacked Nineveh, the great
capital of the feared Assyrians, the same Assyrians who had sacked the northern kingdom of Israel in 721 B.C.?

Yet human extremity is God's opportunity, and human impotence opens the
way for the divine potency to be demonstrated. The people of Israel realized
the truth of a maxim stated by Paul more than five hundred years later, that
"when I am weak, then I am strong" (2 Cor 12:10). For the God of Israel
brought back the captives of Israel, beginning only fifty years after their exile
to Babylon. Nebuchadnezzar's "eternal" kingdom was short lived, and during
the reign of his successors, the power of the Medes and then the Persians
overcame Babylon. When the dust settled, Cyrus the Persian ruled over all, and
he proclaimed a general amnesty in his kingdom and a return of the Jewish
exiles to Judea.

So, contrary to expectations, within the lifetime of some of the original
exiles, they returned to the Promised Land. What joy and rapture accompanied
the returning exiles! It was like a huge parade, a movable feast that returned
to the land. Isaiah 51 captures the unexpected and full joy of the returning
exiles:

The ransomed of the LORD will return.
They will enter Zion with singing;
    everlasting joy will crown their heads.
Gladness and joy will overtake them,
    and sorrow and sighing will flee away. (Is 51:11)

Some such experience and feeling underlies the opening verse of our psalm. "When the LORD brought back the captives to Zion, we were like men who dreamed." It was like smiling an irrepressible smile; the facial muscles relax, the eyes open wide, giddy laughter follows in waves. Our eyes become aware of all things around us, our step is more sprightly, and we look around eagerly as if to say, "It is all too good to be true." We are overcome at first by bewilderment and even a sense of disorientation, but the joy is real because we believe that God has reversed our fortunes. "Our mouths were filled with laughter, our tongues with songs of joy" (v. 2).

The Toil of Weary Grief

Yet the life of the people of Israel and our life doesn't end in surprising joy. We are delighted and swept off our feet by instances of this joy, but we must, however, return to the daily task at hand. We realize that our restoration, though real, is only partial; our life continues in steadfast toil and frequent disappointment. We confess, however, that at the end of this life we will sing songs of joy because of other instances of unexpected good news. The throb of wondering gratitude is inextricably bound up with the toil of weary grief. The rhythms of life, even the healthy Christian life, include waking and sleeping, labor and rest, joy and sorrow, and death and life. Yet the final word will be one of joy, though it be joy even through our tears.

Psalm 126:4 prays for God to continue his goodness to us,

Restore our fortunes, O LORD,
like streams in the Negev.

One restoration of fortunes never satisfies me fully. While it may have been unexpected and truly delightful, and while its effects might remain with us for the rest of our life, we need other restorations. When the psalmist prays for fortunes to be restored "like streams in the Negev," he is longing again for the unexpected. The Negev is the southern Judean desert which is parched and barren at one moment and then, because of sudden rain and flash floods, flooding at the next. Restore again, O Lord, is the prayer. One act of God in our life is never enough. We are so constituted that we need frequent and steady acts of God to buoy us.

We need new acts of restoration because much of life is characterized by steadfast toil and discouragement. We sow some seed and weep as we work. We weep because we often don't see the fruit of our labor. We weep because

200 / LONGING FOR GOD

often it seems in vain. We weep because our toil wearies us. We don't weep and shouldn't weep out of self-pity, but out of a sense that we, because of our finiteness and sin, share in the pain of the world, the world for which Christ died. In our lives there is the constant tension of meeting others' expectations, of pressure from coworkers and supervisors and clients and others. There are the defeats that set us back to square one. There is stagnation, where we go on for seemingly interminable periods without seeing progress or even movement in our lives. The good news of this psalm is that God not only brings the huge reversals of fortune in life, but he also brings the *small* ones. The spiritual truth of labor is like the truth of sowing: unless a grain of wheat dies and falls into the ground, it produces nothing. But when it dies it produces much fruit. If we sow in faith through our labor, we will reap with songs of joy.

The great American novelist Willa Cather said that an author must, as it were, die in her love for her subject in order to be raised to life through the words that then come forth from the pen. We, too, labor by faith. We sow our seed and see the seed, the only thing that can bring life, slip out of our hands. We seem to lose it in the soil, and not until later does it appear to our sight. Just as the seed is transformed by the soil into stalks of wheat, so our tears are transformed through regular toil into moments of transfiguring joy. We expect from God nothing less than another miracle, because God has delivered us so surprisingly in the past.

The word *praise* never appears in Psalm 126. Yet the idea of praise suffuses it. The spirit of Psalm 126 is that of gratitude for unexpected joy, and the boldness of Psalm 126 is the hope, no, the *expectation* that dramatic acts of breathtaking deliverance will happen again. When Abraham was promised a son through Sarah, although Sarah was beyond the age of childbearing, he kept believing and hoping,

> Yet he did not waver through unbelief, . . . being fully persuaded that God had power to do what he had promised. (Rom 4:20-21)

Such is the spirit also of Psalm 126. Won't you be bold enough to ask God for the thing which you fervently desire but which is almost too good to be true? Won't you ask God to bring you the rhythms of *wondering gratitude* and *weary grief* and help you see them as part of the ebb and flow of your life? Won't you ask God to restore your fortunes like the waters of the Negev? Remember, God who has promised is faithful and still wants to bring experiences of sudden joy to us.

Prayer

Living God, who restored the fortunes of your people, restore me today. Bring me out of endless and meaningless toil. Better yet, restore me in the midst of my toil. Bring joy to my life, joy that restores and floods my life, and I will praise you with a full heart. Through Jesus Christ our Lord, Amen.

TWENTY-SIX

◇

PSALM 65

———

TAPPING THE ABUNDANCE OF GOD

For the director of music. A psalm of David. A song.

¹*Praise awaits you, O God, in Zion;*
   to you our vows will be fulfilled.
²*O you who hear prayer,*
   to you all men will come.
³*when we were overwhelmed by sins,*
   you forgave our transgressions.
⁴*Blessed are those you choose*
   and bring near to live in your courts!
We are filled with the good things of your house,
   of your holy temple.

⁵*You answer us with awesome deeds of righteousness,*
   O God our Savior,

the hope of all the ends of the earth
and of the farthest seas,
⁶who formed the mountains by your power,
having armed yourself with strength,
⁷who stilled the roaring of the seas,
the roaring of their waves,
and the turmoil of the nations.
⁸Those living far away fear your wonders;
where morning dawns and evening fades
you call forth songs of joy.

⁹You care for the land and water it;
you enrich it abundantly,
The streams of God are filled with water
to provide the people with grain,
for so you have ordained it.
¹⁰You drench its furrows
and level its ridges;
you soften it with showers
and bless its crops.
¹¹You crown the year with your bounty,
and your carts overflow with abundance.
¹²The grasslands of the desert overflow;
the hills are clothed with gladness.
¹³The meadows are covered with flocks
and the valleys are mantled with grain,
they shout for joy and sing.

*I*f one theme runs consistently through Scripture, it is that God has the capacity and desire to provide all and even more than we need. From the first breath of life in Genesis to the tree of life in Revelation, the Scriptures tell of a God who abundantly bestows good things on his people. Elijah, for instance, was hungry and in extreme want during a famine. God sent him to the widow at

Zarephath, promising that "the jar of flour will not be used up and the jug of oil will not run dry until the day the LORD gives rain on the land" (1 Kings 17:14). The apostle Paul knew all manner of rejection, imprisonment, beatings and shipwrecks but could also say, "I can do everything through him who gives me strength" (Phil 4:13).

God's ability and eagerness to provide for all our needs is a crucial thought for John Calvin in his classic *Institutes of the Christian Religion*. When discussing the nature of the Christian life (Book 3.6-9), Calvin uses the images of bearing the cross or denying oneself to capture the essence of Christian discipleship. By denying ourselves and bearing the cross we imitate our Lord and find our true life. But then, Calvin has a wonderful transition chapter (3.10) in which he argues that God, however, has outfitted the world so remarkably and lavishly that the disciple of Christ ought also to enjoy its abundance. Why did God create hundreds of kinds of birds and thousands of types of flowers, when only a few would suffice? Precisely so that we, his creatures, might share in the divine abundance and creativity. Therefore, for Calvin, the Christian life is, at the same time, a life of bearing the cross *and* luxuriating in the abundant goodness of God. Discipline and joy, denial and satisfaction are flip sides of the multifaceted Christian life.

God's abundance is the theme of a striking novella that was recently made into a movie, *A River Runs Through It*. Set in the rich hills of western Montana in the early decades of the twentieth century, *A River Runs Through It* narrates the story of fishing and faith in the life of a Presbyterian pastor and his two sons. In the book and movie, the waters of the Big Blackfoot River are a metaphor for the abundance of God. They are not only the habitat of the fish and the arena for fly fishermen to learn and demonstrate their art, but they also exert a calming and soothing influence on the human soul. As author Norman Maclean says on the last page,

> In the Arctic half-life of the canyon, all existence fades to a being with my soul and memories and the sounds of the Big Blackfoot River and a four-count rhythm and the hope that a fish will rise.

> Eventually all things merge into one, and a river runs through it.

The abundance of waters suggests the abundance of God.

Abundant Power
The theme of full or abundant power characterizes Psalm 65. This psalm is

written by a person who at times was overwhelmed by his sins (v. 3), but is now overwhelmed by the astonishing power and promises of God (vv. 9-13). At one time the roaring of the seas threatened his life (v. 7); now the full streams carry water which provides nourishment for the crops (v. 9). Waters that once oppressed the author, as in Psalm 69, are now carriers of his very life, like the streams in Psalm 46. A river runs through Psalm 65, and it is a river which brings joy and peace to the soul.

First, God's power is shown in drawing us to himself. Note verse 4:

Blessed are those you choose
and bring near to live in your courts!

Jesus said, "You did not choose me, but I chose you and appointed you to go and bear fruit—fruit that will last" (Jn 15:16). The great mystery of our salvation is that we are inexorably drawn to God, yet we come to him freely and joyfully. The abundant power of God over us is not like the call of the mythological Sirens, who called people off course only to lead them to shipwreck. It is rather a gracious call that puts us on the path to full and joyful service in God's sight.

Second, God's abundant power is evident in the creation and taming of nature. The waters that rage so furiously are brought under control. Thus, also, the stormy and swirling waters of despair that threaten to drown us are brought under control by God. As Jesus said "Peace, be still," to the raging waves of the Sea of Galilee, so God stills the stormy seas of nature and of our troubled lives.

Third, God's abundant power is shown in the songs of joy which we sing:

Those living far away fear your wonders;
where morning dawns and evening fades
you call forth songs of joy. (v. 8)

"You call forth" suggests that the music on our lips is put there by God. Sometimes we find ourselves singing the old, familiar melodies of praise; other times new songs burst from deep within us. Let the Spirit of God call forth the tunes from your heart which will nourish you and others also. What abundant power of God is shed abroad in our hearts!

Abundant Provision

God not only provides a song in our hearts and on our lips; he also makes nature provide abundantly for us. Nature's song and provision, however, is a

silent one. Nature sings by quietly performing its intended function: the grasslands overflow, the crops multiply, the meadows are covered with flocks. Hear
the silence of the provision of God:

You care for the land and water it;
you enrich it abundantly.
The streams of God are filled with water
to provide the people with grain,
for so you have ordained it. (v. 9)

The silent beauty and abundance of nature is reminiscent of the words from
a Christmas carol, "How silently, how silently, the wondrous gift is given."

The abundant provision of God in nature is the foundation for a Christian
approach to ecology. God is the God *of* nature but is not to be identified *with*
nature. Nevertheless, the goodness of God is shown through his provisions in
nature, and God's grandeur and mercy are evident in the seasonal rhythm of
growth and harvest. A Christian approach to nature neither deifies nature nor
subjects it unmercifully to a welter of technological innovations. It sees nature
as the arena of God's silent creative abundance.

The idyllic picture of the rich provisions of nature in Psalm 65 recalls the
seventeenth-century Dutch still lifes or eighteenth-century French landscape
paintings. Though still-life objects and landscapes were originally at the bottom
of the hierarchy of subjects for academic painting (behind such things as mythological or biblical paintings, portraits, and scenes from everyday life), by the
middle of the nineteenth century they had become a principal means for ex-
pressing the glory and care of God. One can almost imagine, after reading
verses 10-11, the work of American still-life painter Severin Roesen, as he
portrays the abundant fruit harvest by a careful reproduction of purple and red
and green grapes, apples or oranges peeled with curled rinds lying beside, half
grapefruit with their yellow and pink fading into each other. Verses 12-13
bring to mind a landscape by Thomas Cole, usually painted from a hill, high
above the action below, capturing the meadows girdled with flocks and the
fresh, green grasslands of the Hudson Valley.

What a glad vista is in this psalm. Nature has clothed herself for her annual
silent concert. We rejoice at the sight, but, even more, we rejoice at the provision of God through nature. Truly God fills the hungry with good things.

But our chorus of uninterrupted praise must be mindful of another note,
which challenges all who will continue to sing praises. Just as abundance pro-

vides the context for praise to God, famine must certainly break God's heart and ought to break the hearts of his people. If, as the Scripture says, the rain falls on the just and the unjust, can't we also believe that famine may come to both the just and the unjust? Is it not then a high calling for Christians, when faced with pictures of starving infants, to try to bring about conditions in that land for praise and abundance? May God through his people care for the land and water—not simply in the well-watered furrows of the Americas or Western Europe, but also for the drought-stricken lands of the African Sahel. May God's people help to provide living streams in all the Negevs of the world. May crops appear through God's gracious power and our inspired efforts. Only then can we sing, without a catch in our throats, the song of unmeasured joy and the praise of the abundance of God's power and provision.

Prayer

I praise you, God, that your hand has been with me, guiding me through all seasons of my restless life. Your power has brought me to you, your strength has stilled my tumults, your voice has given me words to sing. Provide, I pray, for all the people of the world, that starvation would be a thing of the past. Use me, even me, O Lord, to bring the water and food of life to all the world. Through Jesus Christ our Lord, Amen.

TWENTY-SEVEN

◇

PSALM 146

———

PRAISE
FOREVER

¹Praise the LORD.

Praise the LORD, O my soul.
  ²I will praise the LORD all my life;
  I will sing praise to my God as long as I live.

³Do not put your trust in princes,
  in mortal men, who cannot save.
⁴When their spirit departs, they return to the ground;
  on that very day their plans come to nothing.

⁵Blessed is he whose help is the God of Jacob,
  whose hope is in the LORD his God,
⁶the Maker of heaven and earth,
  the sea, and everything in them—

the LORD, who remains faithful forever.
⁷He upholds the cause of the oppressed
and gives food to the hungry.
The LORD sets prisoners free,
⁸the LORD gives sight to the blind,
the LORD lifts up those who are bowed down,
the LORD loves the righteous.
⁹The LORD watches over the alien
and sustains the fatherless and the widow,
but he frustrates the ways of the wicked.

¹⁰The LORD reigns forever,
your God, O Zion, for all generations.

Praise the LORD.

W

e have come a long way on our road to praise. Our basic observation about praise is that praise stems from gratitude—gratitude that God has entered our lives and made us his own. St. Augustine reflects this spirit of gratitude beautifully in his *Confessions*. One of the reasons that Augustine wrote this autobiographical classic was to reflect on why it took him so long to come to a position of faith which he knew to be so evidently true. His heart bursts with thankfulness as he surveys the wonder of God's love, love which let him explore the various intellectual and moral options before him, but then brought him to God with joy.

As we have examined praise of God and its role in our life, we started with reasonable praise (Ps 33), that is, praise rooted in a calm assessment of the truth of God's love for us. Then, we responded to God's love by loving (Ps 116:1: "I love the LORD, for he heard my voice"). The great American theologian Jonathan Edwards stated this latter principle succinctly in his treatise on true virtue. The goal of the Christian life, he said, was *disinterested benevolence*, or what he called, "love to being in general."

Our treatment of praise then turned to praise for various attributes and activities of God. We praise God because of the excellency of his name (Ps 8), because he restores us in ways that are often too good to be true (Ps 126), and because his power and provision overwhelm us (Ps 65). Today we will affirm that God is worthy to be praised forever because he keeps us in all circumstances. We have already met the sentiments of Psalm 146 when we studied Psalm 121, a psalm of trust. But, as one commentator says, though Psalm 146 is "largely colored by earlier songs, it still throbs with fresh emotion." Our prayer today is that we will grasp some of this psalm's fresh emotion so that the glorious words of verse 2 may be ours as well:

I will praise the LORD all my life;
I will sing praise to my God as long as I live.

Many vital thoughts come from this psalm, but we will limit ourselves to two: God who is faithful forever (v. 6) and God who gives sight to the blind (v. 8).

Faithful Forever

The writer contrasts the faithfulness of God with the fickleness of humans:

Do not put your trust in princes,
in mortal men, who cannot save. (v. 3)

The psalm has a profound sense of the ultimate unreliability of human sources of help. Like Jesus who "would not entrust himself" to people "for he knew all men" and "he knew what was in a man" (Jn 2:24-25), so this psalm recognizes the flimsy and illusory character of human reliability. Isaiah recognized as much when he castigated Israel for not putting trust in the Holy One of Israel and relying instead on the deceptively strong forces of Egypt (Is 31:1). Compared with the surety of God's faithfulness, even the strongest human bulwark is weak.

Praise is due to God because he is

the Maker of heaven and earth,
the sea, and everything in them—
the LORD, who remains faithful forever. (v. 6)

Biblically speaking, to remain faithful forever means that without God's knowledge not a hair can fall from our heads. To remain faithful forever means that God cannot deny himself, that he will fulfill his promises and that he will continue to love and deliver his people. To remain faithful forever means that God is working for good in our life, even if at times we cannot see where we are going or even where we are.

As we have learned, God is faithful to his *promises*. No biblical person experienced this more powerfully than Abraham. Promised a progeny as numerous as the stars of the heavens (Gen 12:1-3), Abraham lived childless for many years. He saw his own generative power diminish, and his wife was beyond the age of childbearing. He thought that the promise of God for descendants might be fulfilled through a slave of his house or the son of a slave woman. Yet this was not to be the case. Desperation and uncertainty must surely have stalked him as he knew that with each passing day his capacity to have a son decreased. Yet, as Paul says,

Against all hope, Abraham in hope believed. . . . Without weakening in faith he faced the fact that his body was as good as dead. . . . Yet he did not waver through unbelief regarding the promise of God, but was strengthened in his faith and gave glory to God, being fully persuaded that God had power to do what he had promised. (Rom 4:18-21)

Finally, after seemingly interminable years of waiting,

The LORD was gracious to Sarah as he had said, and the LORD did for Sarah what he had promised. Sarah became pregnant and bore a son to Abraham in his old age, at the very time God had promised him. (Gen 21:1-2)

God is faithful to his promises because God is faithful to his *people*. As an early Christian creed has it, "If we are faithless, he will remain faithful, for he cannot disown himself" (2 Tim 2:13). God is faithful because he is tied to us, bound to us "for better or for worse." The three young men in the fiery furnace of the book of Daniel found this to be true. As the flames licked high and they were thrown into the fire, they, surprisingly, did not burn because there was another person in the fire with them, "and the fourth looks like a son of the gods," as the Babylonians said (Dan 3:25). God's presence with his people in the extremities of life is symbolic of God's presence with us in the routines of life. If God brings life out of almost certain death or destruction, he can and will redeem us from our afflictions. Though the flames burn hotter, though the promise of God seems unrealizable because of our age, infirmity or position in life, God remains faithful forever, and God will do it. So we praise God, who is faithful forever.

Sight to the Blind

When Psalm 146 says that "the LORD gives sight to the blind" (v. 8), it surely has a physical *and* a spiritual connotation. When Jesus proclaimed the year of the Lord's favor (Lk 4:19), he quoted Isaiah 61, where his vision included a proclamation of freedom for the prisoners and "recovery of sight for the blind" (4:18). Jesus himself gave sight to the sightless in more than one way. He healed the eyes of the flesh and the eyes of the soul. The continuing work of Jesus in our world today includes both kinds of healing.

First, it includes the work of physical healing or physical liberation. If God "upholds the cause of the oppressed and gives food to the hungry" (v. 7), can I do any less? If God "watches over the alien and sustains the fatherless and the widow" (v. 9), can I ignore their plight? My God is not a God of the status quo. My God is not one who shields his eyes from injustice. If this God is my help (v. 5), what can I do but serve those God pledges to help?

The work of Jesus in the world also includes the work of spiritual liberation. For God to bring about spiritual liberation or remove my spiritual blindness means that he enables me to see things from a new perspective. The pressures on me are strong not to see things anew or afresh. I become committed to certain experiences of truth or specific words or phrases. I have my favorite texts, hymns, doctrines, writers and people. I like things a certain way and am loath to see things differently. I become invested in the status quo. It gives me predictability and faithful rhythms. But sometimes the grooves of life become the ruts of life, and I need someone to open my eyes so I can see things differently.

In the past few years we Americans have been challenged to see things differently. The famine in Somalia has challenged our political and moral sensibility. Politically we may be engaging in an effort where there is little "payoff" for America—there are few markets in Somalia. Morally, however, we see the importance of stopping the inevitable loss of life through famine and warfare.

The confirmation hearings for Judge Clarence Thomas to the Supreme Court have opened many Americans' eyes to the issue of sexual harassment. Or again, the recent release of *Malcolm X*, a film by Spike Lee, challenges us to reexamine the career of an African-American activist from the 1960s.

In many ways we are being challenged to see too many things anew. All around us are reinterpretations, whether it is Tom Peters, the management guru now celebrating "creative chaos" in companies, or Benny Schmidt, the former president of Yale, trying to reform American secondary education, or voices from a number of places that would like to see us reexamine the role of women and homosexual people in the military.

We often are so reluctant to see things anew because so many of the things we are challenged to see in a different way strike us as strange or different or even repulsive. The people we are called upon to serve are often those with whom we would not otherwise associate. Yet the God we praise is a God of compassion. He is not a God who simply wants us to repeat the old patterns of life. He is leading us into a new and uncertain future. The constant certainty, though, is that God will remain faithful forever. Our changing reality comes from God's opening our eyes to see things differently. Let us praise this God as long as we live, for our God is forever faithful and forever opening our eyes to see wonderful and challenging things in his Word and in his world.

Prayer

O Lord my God, my security is in you alone. The princes of the earth promise me easy prosperity and effortless change, yet you give me your eternal faithfulness. Open my eyes to behold you and your world afresh; fill me with vision and desire, that I may see as you see and act as you would have me act. Through Jesus Christ our Lord, Amen.

TWENTY-EIGHT

◇

PSALM 100

SHOUTING FOR JOY

A psalm. For giving thanks.

¹*Shout for joy to the LORD, all the earth.*
  ²*Worship the LORD with gladness;*
  come before him with joyful songs.
³*Know that the LORD is God.*
  It is he who made us, and we are his;
  we are his people, the sheep of his pasture.
⁴*Enter his gates with thanksgiving*
  and his courts with praise;
  give thanks to him and praise his name.
⁵*For the LORD is good and his love endures forever;*
  his faithfulness continues through all generations.

A *new note is sounded in this psalm that will carry us to the end of our* songs of praise in this book. That note is the invitation to all people of the earth to come into God's house and praise him. As God's purpose unfolds in our life, we begin to praise God for who he *is* and what he has *done.* Our next step of faith is to exhort every human being to join us in our song of praise. This new theme will receive its fullest expression in our last study (Ps 150), when the psalmist commands all of creation to praise God.

It is appropriate that we think about and celebrate the hope that someday every creature will offer praise to God. Such a hope takes our eyes off ourselves and puts our life into proper perspective. God certainly loves us, but we are only one small part of the plan God is working out for all of creation. Indeed, Scripture spends more time describing God's plan of redemption for all people than his act of salvation for any one individual.

For example, in 1 Corinthians 15:20-28, Paul describes his view of the last days. Christ, at the end of time, will hand over the kingdom to God the Father after destroying all contrary dominions, authorities and powers. Some day, all things will be visibly subordinate to God and in that day, "every knee should bow, in heaven and on earth and under the earth, and every tongue confess that Jesus Christ is Lord, to the glory of God the Father" (Phil 2:10-11).

Yet Psalm 100 also stands in continuity with the other psalms of praise we have explored. Familiar phrases abound in Psalm 100, and many scholars see Psalm 100 as a moving summary statement of thoughts contained in Psalms 93—99. We have already explored the themes of joy (v. 1), thanksgiving (v. 4) and God's enduring faithfulness (v. 5). Psalm 100 is, thus, a psalm that has a foot in two worlds: it celebrates the virtue of God who saves *individuals,* and it challenges us to see God as the Lord of all, who will not be satisfied until *all the world* recognizes his dominion.

Let us then approach this brief psalm and see its familiarity and its newness as we sharpen our songs of praise to God. We will examine the familiar thought that we belong to God (v. 3), and the new thought that all the earth will someday praise God joyfully (v. 1).

We Belong to God

One of the issues that Judy and I (Bill) discussed when our children were young was when they would be permitted to take Communion. Although Judy and I had grown up in churches that discouraged children from taking Communion, we felt that we would permit our children to do so as soon as they had a basic understanding of the Christian faith. I searched my soul and felt that this understanding would be for them to say, "Jesus is mine." I observed my children and saw that they had a very clear understanding of what was "mine" by the time they were two or three. I felt that this basic concept of possessing or belonging was one of the first things they could articulate that had a rich biblical meaning.

With this in mind, I reread Psalm 100:3 and was overwhelmed by its simple and clear affirmation:

It is he who made us, and we are his.

Every time I say or hear this verse, I think of my three-year-old daughter saying, "Jesus is mine." The sentiments are not identical. "Jesus is mine" emphasizes our ownership and initiative in the life of faith. "I am his" points to my dependence on him and obedience to him. Yet they both stress the intimacy and permanence of the relationship between us and God, and it was this that interested me as I spoke with my daughter.

I knew that even though she didn't understand much of what her words meant, she knew enough to confound the proud of this world. I also knew that in my entire spiritual journey I would never exhaust the meaning of that brief affirmation.

Her confession, "Jesus is mine," served as a reminder to me that as disciples of Jesus Christ, we belong to God. The Song of Songs has it, "My lover is mine and I am his" (2:16). Paul expresses the same thought over and over again in his epistles. On several occasions he will call himself a servant of the Lord. He teaches us in 1 Corinthians, "You are not your own; you were bought at a price" (6:19-20). He says in a passage of remarkable depth and intensity, "I have been crucified with Christ and I no longer live, but Christ lives in me" (Gal 2:20).

Because we belong to God, God knows us. Our desires and longings and secrets are not hidden from him. So often we think that we see and understand things so clearly, and that, therefore, we don't need God's help to clarify things for us. Yet our hearing is impaired and our vision occluded. God is the one who made the eye and the ear. He knows how they function, and he alone can remove the darkness from our vision and the deafness from our ears. God knows us thoroughly. He knows we belong to him. He has given us Jesus Christ to live and experience the depth of human emotion, yet without sin, and so he not only saves us but also encourages and empowers us in our daily battles of life. It is God who made us; it is to him alone that we belong.

We belong to God and he belongs to us. Our paths have crossed, so to speak. Though they remain two paths, we believe, by faith, that they are growing closer together each day. Every morning as we arise, then, let us say these words from the psalm and personalize them: "I am yours." Everyone has time to say such a prayer. When the pace at work is intense, why not stop, take a moment and say, "Lord, I am yours." When relationships with friends or spouse are threatened, why not say, "I am yours, O Lord." Knowledge of *who* we are is rooted in knowledge of *whose* we are. Our greatest declaration is not one of independence but of dependence. We shout for joy and thankfully praise God because he has made us his.

Though I have read Psalm 100 as a personal confession, I can also see it as the cry of praise of the entire community of faith. The church's shout of praise is more robust and enduring than our personal cry. *Its* shout buoys me when I am weak, and it leads me when I am strong. My shout is caught up in the shout of the people of God.

All the Earth

The Psalms are written by ancient Israelites. For most of their life in antiquity, the Israelites were oppressed by enemies. If that is national experience, it would be difficult to develop an *inclusive* theology, that is, a theology that includes your enemies as recipients of God's grace. Indeed, portions of the Old Testament have extremely negative views about some outsiders. But occasionally, as in this psalm, the psalmist breaks out of his national context and experience and longs for *all people* to know his God.

> Shout for joy to the LORD, all the earth.
> Worship the LORD with gladness;
> come before him with joyful songs. (*vv. 1-2*)

The feeling I get as I study this and the two following psalms is that the psalmist's and God's joy cannot be full until "outsiders" are singing the praise of God. His cup of joy will not overflow until the Gentiles enter God's gates with thanksgiving. Normally the Gentiles were prohibited from entering the temple confines. The God of Israel was to be worshiped by the people of Israel. But in this moment of inspiration, the psalmist catches a vision of how the *walls* of the temple might become *windows* and how the court of Israel could become the court of all nations.

This psalm is remarkable because its vision of a unified humanity worshipping God effectively overcomes the reality of ethnic particularism. This is a picture that Israel in its day and we in ours need to see. God's ultimate vision is a humanity united in his praise. God is the one who invites *all* to share his bounty. His goodness is available to *all* people. God will break down the walls of his own house so that all may feast at his table and enjoy his presence.

There is no more urgent message for our world today than this. Many scholars see resurgent tribalism as the most powerful reality in our day. Tribal wars break out in the former Soviet Union, in Yugoslavia, in African countries. We all feel as if we are most safe when we retreat into our homogeneous ghettos and identify only with our old tribal alliances. Our world needs strong people who will practice the opposite: not necessarily strive to eliminate all differences among people, but to build upon difference and distinction as we construct a great unified house of praise for all nations. May it be our desire to have our lives be as inclusive of others as the Scriptures say that God is inclusive of humanity. May Psalm 100 get under our skin when we say the words "all the earth"; and may it beckon us to work for that day when all people shall praise God the Lord.

Prayer

O Lord my God, break me out of the narrow confines of my life and faith. Give me the courage to know that I am yours; give me honesty and humility so that when I long for all the earth to praise you, I may be willing to help that become a reality. Through Jesus Christ our Lord, Amen.

TWENTY-NINE

◇

PSALM 67

IN
EVER-GROWING
CIRCLES

For the director of music. With stringed instruments. A psalm. A song.

[1]*May God be gracious to us and bless us*
and make his face shine upon us,

[2]*that your ways may be known on earth,*
your salvation among all nations.

[3]*May the peoples praise you, O God;*
may all the peoples praise you.
[4]*May the nations be glad and sing for joy,*
for you rule the peoples justly
and guide the nations of the earth.

⁵*May the peoples praise you, O God;*
may all the peoples praise you.

⁶*Then the land will yield its harvest,*
and God, our God, will bless us.
⁷*God will bless us,*
and all the ends of the earth will fear him.

I *n the last two studies of this book we will see how the Scriptures invite us and* all the world to sing our song of praise in ever-widening circles. When more people are added to the chorus, the sound becomes richer and fuller. Praise is proper for the individual believer and the community of faith and every human being. Psalm 67 emphasizes even more strongly than Psalm 100 the longing for all the world's people to praise God.

Praise is soothing medicine for sick souls and a hurting world. We find the fulfillment of our life in praise to God; for praise, in the final analysis, is our way of saying yes to life. We have seen that it is so easy to live in the pain of the past or in the lack of trust and cynicism that has become almost second nature to us or in the selfishness of the human heart curved in on itself. It is so easy to yield to the negative weight of others' comments or painful circumstances that dog us. Praise, though, draws us out of ourselves and forces us to look heavenward. Like the soaring nave of a Gothic cathedral, praise lifts our vision upward, to confess that God alone is the source of all our blessings. Praise helps us probe beneath the veneer or the externalism of modern life and recognize the glory of God in speckled and brindled and striped things, as did the nineteenth-century British poet Gerard Manley Hopkins.

When Isaiah looked upon the glory of God in the sanctuary, he was overwhelmed by his vision:

Holy, holy, holy is the LORD Almighty;
    the whole earth is full of his glory. (Is 6:3)

If only we had eyes to see the abundant beauty and manifestations of God everywhere. May our prayer be that God will open our eyes to see what is already plainly in view so that the language of praise will tumble from our lips as the experience of gratitude fills our hearts.

Psalm 67 helps us praise God for the expansive, and often hidden, works of God. One of the most memorable sermons of my seminary days was on this psalm. My professor of missions probably chose Psalm 67 as a text because it is a missionary psalm. It is driven by an intense longing for the earth to be filled someday with the glory of God as the waters cover the sea. My professor had been a missionary to the Muslim world for thirty years before he began to teach at the seminary. All who know something about foreign missions know that evangelism among the Muslims is usually considered a most difficult and even futile undertaking. As he preached on this text, however, his face lit up—with gratitude, longing and humility—at the realization that, for some inexplicable reason, the God of the universe had chosen us to be the bearers of the good news. Despite being expelled from Afghanistan in the early 1970s, he was grateful to God that he could carry the story of salvation among the nations. He was confident that God's hidden work was going on in that country even as it closed its borders to the work of Christian missions.

The major focus of Psalm 67 is the desire for all nations to praise God for his graciousness. Yet the psalm begins with a longing for God's blessing on the community of faith. These two themes, starting with the latter, will be the focus of our meditation. Our hope is that through this psalm we may more fully understand and grasp the worldwide nature of our Christian discipleship.

God Be Gracious

The psalm begins with a longing for God's blessing:

May God be gracious to us and bless us
and make his face shine upon us.

I am so glad for two things in this psalm; first, that the psalmist starts with a desire for blessing, and second, that the desire for personal blessing only takes up the first and last verses, while the blessing on the nations occupies the heart of the psalm. The biblical pattern is that God blesses us so that we may be instruments of this blessing to others, and that they will then return their gratitude to God.

The consistent message of the Scriptures is that God takes pleasure in blessing his people. God's way is to make his people strong, even though their strength might need to be developed in the valley of the shadow of death. The particular yearning for God's graciousness in verse 1 is based on the great

benediction of Aaron before the people of Israel, a benediction that is still part
of our worship today:

The LORD bless you
and keep you;
the LORD make his face shine upon you
and be gracious to you;
the LORD turn his face toward you
and give you peace. (Num 6:24-26)

The phrase "make his face shine upon you" is particularly vivid. It means that
it is our strongest hope that God would illumine our lives with the wonderful,
radiant power of his Word. As Paul says,

For God, who said, "Let light shine out of darkness," made his light shine in our
hearts to give us the light of the knowledge of the glory of God in the face of Christ.
(2 Cor 4:6)

We bask in and bear the light of God's blessing to all the world.

All the People

Only if we give our blessings away to others can we be fully blessed. Blessings
clutched closely to our chest neither warm or comfort us nor strengthen or
uplift others. But shared blessings bring even more. Have you ever noticed that
after a truly successful venture people who have put their heart and soul into
that venture usually claim that they got more out of it than they gave? Isn't
this an illustration of the point that an unselfish desire to share the blessings
of God brings blessings to all—giver and recipient alike?

One word dominates the psalm—the little word *all.* The phrases "all nations" (v. 2), or "all the peoples" (vv. 3, 5), or "all the ends of the earth" (v.
7) appear four times. This psalm is directed out to the ends of the earth. It
has a heart for all the people of the world. In placing so much emphasis on
"all the world," this psalm shows that it is an arrow shot from the quiver of
God. The Scriptures teach us, time and again, that God will not be pleased until
people from east and west and south and north sit down and have a meal
together in the kingdom of God.

So this intense and large-hearted psalm invites all people to the great festival
of praising God. Somehow, in God's plan, the party cannot go on until all have
arrived. It is like the Thanksgiving dinner or Christmas banquet that is most
joyfully celebrated when all are present. When everyone is in the room, from

ages two to ninety-two, even though there may only be one quick moment before the reign of chaos threatens to return, the picture of all together becomes frozen in the mind's eye. To the Christian, it is a harbinger and a yearning for that great day when all the people of God will he gathered together in an eternal banquet.

Psalm 67 teaches us that it is neither right nor scriptural for the blessings of God to stop with us. The vision of inclusive praise means that the song to the Father and to the Lamb will be sung by

a great multitude that no one could count, from every nation, tribe, people and language, standing before the throne and in front of the Lamb. (Rev 7:9)

The crying need today is for Christians who long to extend the blessings of God to all the earth. The time is ripe for Christians who understand that what they are doing in extending this blessing is working in partnership with people all over the world so that *their* lives may be full and *their* songs of praise might be natural to them.

The mission of the church in our day is to promote teams of caring people who are not so concerned with keeping track of which missions have brought more people to Christian faith as with helping each people find their own voice in praising the God who made and sustains them. Now is the time, more than ever, for us to develop a global consciousness. As the invitation is sent out to all nations and peoples to join the great festival of eternal praise, the invitation is sent to us to see ourselves as world Christians—Christians whose hearts should yearn to see the blessings of God reach every corner of the earth. Then we will be able to add our voice to the multilingual chorus of praise that will be fully satisfying to God.

Prayer

O Lord our God, you have blessed me with so many things of this life and of eternity. I am strong through your blessings, but my heart yearns to be kindled to share the riches of these blessings with the world. May I give myself for the life of the world so that all may sing your psalms with heartfelt joy. Through Jesus Christ our Lord, Amen.

THIRTY

◇

PSALM 150

PRAISE AS A WAY
OF LIFE

¹Praise the LORD.

Praise God in his sanctuary;
  praise him in his mighty heavens.
²Praise him for his acts of power;
  praise him for his surpassing greatness.
³Praise him with the sounding of the trumpet,
  praise him with the harp and lyre,
⁴praise him with tambourine and dancing,
  praise him with the strings and flute,
⁵praise him with the clash of cymbals,
  praise him with resounding cymbals.

⁶Let everything that has breath praise the LORD.

Praise the LORD.

W*e come to the end of our book with the hope that this is only the* beginning of your journey with the Psalms. We have chosen thirty psalms to explore under the four movements of longing, distress, trust and praise. The unexpected joy we have discovered in this book is that as we have studied these thirty psalms, many of the other 120 have also taken on a fresh meaning for us. That is, we feel that the fourfold division of longing, distress, trust and praise is a helpful tool for entering into the heart of the entire psalter. So as you finish reading this book, think of how you can continue your study with the tools that we have provided here.

You may discover that several other psalms cannot simply be put into these categories, but that these categories can help you see the issues of life and faith more clearly as you study them. You may also discover that new categories are needed. For example, we did not have time to explore the great history psalms (such as Psalms 78; 105—107), which talk about God's work in the past as a prelude to his work today. We did not study the great psalms of the law (Psalms 1; 19; 119), which stress that our blessedness is in the mastery of and meditation upon the Scriptures.

So view this book as an invitation to your own further study, as an invitation to make Psalms a lifelong partner that challenges, rebukes, encourages, elevates and incites to balance and service in Christ's name. The rhythms, cadences and precise formulations of the psalms will become a precious asset for your Christian discipleship. The psalms will become friends and constant companions; they continue to probe and elevate us and to clear our way in the turbulence of a century's turning.

The psalter and this book end with praise. We have experienced tears and groans, fainting faith and failed aspirations, faltering trust and feeble hope, yet we have also seen victory over the pit and resolutions to trust again and open-hearted and radiant praise to God. We have learned more than ever that praise should be the direction and goal of life. Just as exercise and proper diet are foundational for healthy bodies, so praise is the fundamental regimen for meaningful spiritual life.

When we praise God, we thank him and we receive his gift of life. When we praise God our eyes are opened to see the world in new ways. Our senses become heightened, our energy is enhanced and our connection to all of life becomes more vital. Our greatest fear in praising God, that it would mean a denial of the pain of life or an abandonment of critical thinking, is, ultimately, a fear that can be overcome. Praise permits pain and praise permits critical thinking. But praise refuses to let pain put the final interpretation on life. Praise refuses to let critical thinking and criticism be the last word on any human or divine phenomenon. When we praise God we state our desire to affirm life in the midst of threatening death. It is our way of saying yes to life, even when the temptations to give in to negativity are immense. By our praising God, by our affirming life, even when it is difficult to do so, we find, mysteriously, that life has a way of affirming us. The Scriptures teach that we find our true life in losing it; when we are "lost" in wonder, love and praise, we discover that the life we live is given back to us.

Praise of God, then, is ultimately a habit or discipline of the Christian life. By it we say yes to what we know of God, and we receive each new day as a precious gift where opportunities and possibilities await us. By praising we discover that people are more willing to open their lives to us. We discover the true shape of the world's needs. And as we discover those needs and are sensitized to others through praise, we find our call to serve God in this world. Our roots, then, are in praise to God and in affirming life wherever we encounter it. Keep on believing in God and in people, for God still believes in you.

Psalm 150 adds the final "Amen" to the swelling chorus of praise. It is among the briefest psalms of praise, but its grandeur is in its brevity. We are exhorted to praise God thirteen times in six verses. The end of the Psalms and the end of life is found in praise, but only *after* longing and distress and trust are explored. Then here we have the clear, unambiguous and final note of unmeasured praise. We cannot measure the praise of Psalm 150. But we can, in closing, indicate three things from the text that will serve us as good words of dismissal and benediction. These three are praise of God everywhere, for all things and by all means.

Everywhere
> Praise God in his sanctuary;
>   praise him in his mighty heavens. (v. 1)

In heaven and on earth the praise of God resounds. Praise God in the holy places of life, in the sacred spaces of your world. But praise God also everywhere under the broad sky of heaven. Perhaps the psalmist is addressing angels as well as people when he says, "Praise him in his mighty heavens." The scope of praise is wide indeed. From every shore and in every setting the praise of God should arise. You are never too far away from God to praise. Earth sounds and heaven responds with the echoing chorus. Add your voice to the strain, feeble as it may be, wherever you are. Say, "I praise you, O God, for you are my life-giver and my compassionate friend. I will praise you as long as I breathe."

For All Things

In Psalm 150:2 we praise God for his "acts of power" and his "surpassing greatness." Since God's power and greatness are displayed everywhere, we interpret this verse to mean that we should praise God for all things. Everything in and of itself is not good; everything in the light of God's purpose works for good. Praising God in all circumstances, even when it seems contrary to wisdom and good sense, is the best avenue to gain understanding and wisdom about the complexities of life. Praising God for all things is, therefore, an essential element in our strategy of living. Both of us say this to you with renewed conviction because, during the writing of this book, we have experienced some of the distresses and struggles that have made trust and praise difficult for us. Praise does not come naturally to either of us; we have learned, through loss and foolishness, that praise, however, is the most powerful ingredient to bring order, rhythm and a sense of continually growing meaning to our lives. But our praise must not be *selective* praise—it must be a habit, almost an instinct, to respond to life with the open arms of affection and praise. Won't you make that your solemn pledge and habitual action, to praise God for the "mixed plaid" of life which is yours?

By All Means

Finally, we praise God with every means at our disposal. In Psalm 150 the means described are musical instruments. But think of other ways to praise God, vocally or silently. Can you shout? Praise God with a shout. Can you paint? Praise God through art. Can you garden? Make your garden a silent symphony of praise. May you and every creature, in heaven and on earth, everything that breathes, make the choice of praise today—everywhere, in all circumstances, by all means. And let our hearts be filled thereby with all the fullness of God. May your heart yearn to do and see the right established. May you have strength to see the distress of life as a means for your own strengthening and growth. May you learn anew to trust God. May your lips and your heart sing with praise to him. May the Psalms bring rhythm and grace to your life!

Prayer
Send me out, O Lord my God, with a brimming heart, to praise you in all instances and to serve you in this world that you love so much. May praise be ever in my mind and on my lips. May praise open the secrets of life for me and help me discover myself, others and you in fresh and dynamic ways. Through Jesus Christ our Lord, Amen.

Questions for Study and Reflection

Part 1: Longing for God

Psalm 63: Longing for God

1. If you were to make a list of what people yearn for today, what would be on that list? Why do people yearn for these things?

2. What are the central objects of *your* desire? Why do you desire them?

3. What makes you lose your spiritual balance or focus?

4. Do you have more of a tendency to become consumed by good things and so become burned out or to become frozen in unconcern and withdraw from life?

5. Do you believe that God can help you bring to your life a greater sense of balance and harmony? Why?

Part 2: Living with Distress

Psalm 102: Alone

1. What do each of the following words mean to you: 1) loneliness, 2) rejection, 3) abandonment? Do you ever feel that one of these words describes your condition? Why?

2. This psalm is about someone who has lost his way in midlife. Why do people (you) lose their (your) way in midlife? What resources do they (you) draw upon to try to get back on the right path?

3. Are you afraid of dying? What do you fear about it?

4. What do you think about when you lay awake at night? Why do you think you are unable to sleep?

5. What do you do when you feel lonely? Is there a difference for you between being alone and being lonely? How do you think your life could be made more whole or complete?

Psalm 130: Waiting

1. When have you experienced the depths of life? Do you feel that you are the cause of your own depths?

2. How have you approached God when you were in the depths of your life? Do you

pray calmly? confidently? desperately? sullenly? not at all?

3. For what have you been waiting or are you waiting? Do you find waiting an easy experience? Do you have a tendency to "take things into your own hands" or "see how they develop"? Why? Give some examples.

4. What do you do in the time between, that is, after you have called to God from your depths and before the deliverance comes? How do you handle the "in-between" times?

Psalm 51: Guilty

1. In this psalm, David feels guilty for an action in his past. As you search your past, what emotions arise? For what are you grateful and for what do you feel guilty?

2. How do you make your past a source of strength rather than weakness for you today? Does the past ever rise up and accuse you? How and in what circumstances?

3. Describe three incidents or people from your past which have exerted a profound influence on you.

4. We maintained that one of the reasons David pursued Bathsheba was that he was out of rhythm and felt weak, and that he wanted an experience to make himself feel strong. When do you feel weak? What do you do to try to regain your sense of strength?

Psalm 88: The Abyss

1. Psalm 88 confronts the darkest depths of life. Have you ever descended to the abyss?

2. Have you ever been afraid of what you might do to yourself or to someone else? Are you afraid to answer this question?

3. How have you been able to maintain your faith when all you can see is darkness? Why do you believe that God is there even in the darkness?

4. How has light started to shine in your darkness? Where does the light come from?

Part 3: Learning to Trust God

Psalm 90: Our Eternal Home

1. We claimed that because we have felt betrayed in life, it is difficult for us to trust God and that "we must work through several issues before learning to trust God again with our lives." What are some of the things that make it difficult for you to trust God?

2. Why do parents teach their children not to trust people? Can you trust God with your life without having a basic attitude of trust toward people?

3. Psalm 90 stresses the great gulf between God and people. God is eternal, we are transient; God is perfect, we sin; God is without limit, we are limited. How does the great gap between us and God help or hinder us in our quest to trust him?

4. What are some practical things you have done or can do to increase your trust of God and people?

Psalm 121: Trust for the Journey

1. Our lives in Christ can be likened to a *battle* or to a *journey*. How is the Christian

life like a battle? How like a journey? Does either of these two have an appeal to you? Which one?

2. What are the sources of help which people seek today? What kind of help do these sources provide? How is it true that the Lord is your keeper?

3. On the way to Jerusalem the pilgrim of Psalm 121 faces many obstacles. What are the obstacles you face today? Which ones have you overcome? How do you face your present obstacles?

4. What role have friends played for you in your Christian life? Do you have few and close friends or hundreds of acquaintances or no friends at all? Is it difficult or easy for you to form friendships?

Psalm 37: Don't Worry—Learn to Trust!

1. We said that Michael Jordan was able to let his own rhythms merge with the rhythms of the game, rather than try to impose himself on the game. What does this mean to you? Are you able to let your rhythms merge with the "rhythms of the game"? Why or why not?

2. We stated that worry and trust are incompatible. What are your worries? Why do these things worry you? What are your strategies for overcoming your worries?

3. We said that "preoccupation with things outside of our control leads to our planning and doing of evil." How might this be so? Has it ever been true for you?

4. What are some synonyms of *trust*? What is *your* special word for trust?

Psalm 40: Out of the Pit

1. What does trust mean to you? Whom do you trust? Why?

2. Has someone ever betrayed your trust? Did you examine your feelings when this occurred?

3. One of our sentences in this chapter reads, "Learning how to trust God is one of the most difficult, yet central, issues of the religious life." Do you agree with this statement? How is it difficult to trust God? Why is trust so central?

4. When do you sing? What do you sing? What does singing do for you? How are singing and trusting God related for you?

Part 4: Loving to Praise God

Psalm 33: Reasonable Praise

1. What does praising God mean to you? Does praising God come easily for you?

2. Does willingness to praise people have anything to do with our ability to praise God?

3. We maintained that "an attitude of gratitude or a mood of thankfulness is at the heart of what the Scriptures mean when they urge us to praise God." How do you cultivate an "attitude of gratitude" in your life? Can people tell when your expressions of gratitude are insincere? What are obstacles to your being grateful to God for your life?

4. Are the words *calm* and *praise* contradictory for you? Does praising God mean the abandonment of your feelings or intellect? Why or why not?

Psalm 116: The Joy of Being Heard
1. What are some instances in your life when you really felt as if someone had heard your concern? What did you feel when you knew you had been heard?
2. What does it mean to love God? What is the role of feeling and intellect in the love of God and people? Because love is such an imprecise word, of what value is it for us in describing our relationship to God or other people?
3. Is it possible to love creation or show love in general to the world?
4. What particular activities has your love of some person or thing led you to perform?

Psalm 126: Dreaming
1. Citizens of the United States have never had to experience another country taking over our land. Since conquest by another and exile far from home was a reality for the Jewish people, how can we who are Americans hope to understand their sense of loss or sadness at conquest and exile?
2. We said, in regard to Israel's experience, that "human extremity is God's opportunity, and human impotence opens the way for divine potency to be demonstrated." Has this been true for you? When have you felt that God's strength has carried you through life?
3. Why is one example of unexpected good news never enough for us?
4. Does the throb of wondering gratitude ever become the daily reality of our lives? Do we always experience, along with it, the toil of weary grief? Are things getting better for you as you get older? Why or why not?

Psalm 65: Tapping the Abundance of God
1. How can we celebrate and gratefully receive the abundance of God without being too materialistic?
2. Where have you seen the abundance of God demonstrated in your life? Do you believe that God desires to bless your life abundantly?
3. What is your responsibility as a Christian to people in this country or in other locations who do not have abundance? Do you rush to help? Give your money at the church? Pray for the people? Avoid the issue?
4. If God's abundance is such a striking and common theme in the Scriptures, why do you think this abundance is so unequally distributed on earth?